NEERAJ CHOPRA

Arjun Singh Kadian is an academic and policy professional working from offices in Haryana and Delhi. A geologist by training, he graduated from Hansraj College, University of Delhi, and received his master's degree with a gold medal. In addition to teaching, Arjun has worked at the Haryana chief minister's office and travelled widely across the region to understand the nuances of the state. Arjun is an alumnus of the Observer Research Foundation and ZEIT-Stiftung. He is also a fellow at Konrad-Adenauer-Stiftung. Arjun is also involved with projects like Indic Academy, Rath Foundation and has initiated the Haryana Thinkers Forum. He has presented Haryana's views on multiple platforms, both in print and digital.

Also by the author

Land of the Gods: The Story of Haryana

NEERAJ CHOPRA
FROM PANIPAT TO THE PODIUM

ARJUN SINGH KADIAN

Published by
Rupa Publications India Pvt. Ltd 2022
7/16, Ansari Road, Daryaganj
New Delhi 110002

Sales Centres:
Allahabad Bengaluru Chennai
Hyderabad Jaipur Kathmandu
Kolkata Mumbai

Copyright © Arjun Singh Kadian 2022

All rights reserved.
No part of this publication may be reproduced, transmitted,
or stored in a retrieval system, in any form or by any means,
electronic, mechanical, photocopying, recording or otherwise,
without the prior permission of the publisher.

The views and opinions expressed in this book are the author's own and the
facts are as reported by him which have been verified to the extent possible,
and the publishers are not in any way liable for the same.

ISBN: 978-93-5520-172-0

First impression 2022

10 9 8 7 6 5 4 3 2 1

The moral right of the author has been asserted.

This book is sold subject to the condition that it shall not,
by way of trade or otherwise, be lent, resold, hired out, or otherwise
circulated, without the publisher's prior consent, in any form of binding or
cover other than that in which it is published.

Contents

Introduction — vii

1. 2020 Tokyo Olympics — 1
2. Haryana and History — 17
3. Starting Young — 30
4. En Route to Panipat — 47
5. Becoming a Pro — 67
6. Soaring High — 85
7. To the Olympics — 114
8. Man with the Golden Arm — 149

Epilogue — 181

Acknowledgments — 190

Introduction

My debut book, *Land of the Gods—The Story of Haryana*, was then in its final stages. A great deal of effort went into the details. The book took years of efforts—I naturally was a little anxious ensuring everything fell into place. I remember a close friend, who hailed from UP, saying, '*Arjun Sir, aap Haryana ko leke thoda zyada emotional ho!* (Arjun Sir, you are a bit too emotional about Haryana).' I could not help but laugh and then told him, 'I guess I am. It's this state and this country which has given me a direction of service. I also firmly believe that I am in a position—both with capabilities and understanding—to give back to the state which may yield results in near future.' He responded in characteristic style, '*Done hai, Sir. Aap se poori hope hai* (I get it, Sir. We have high hopes from you).'

But the journey had its own hurdles. My first draft had around one and half lakh words. It was a lot considering that I wanted to write a popular non-fiction book. However, I was also convinced that in order to tell the modern story of Haryana, I would have to set a context and then build up from there. Further, in order to make it an interesting and pacy read, I had to delete many parts and bring the final draft to around 90,000 words.

As a consequence, many stories of contemporary Haryana and high achieving Haryanvis had to be cut short. I was naturally a little upset. However, as a first time author I trusted my publishers and mentors. In order to pacify my inner spirit of exploration and understanding Haryana more, I began planning how to write the modern story of Haryana in more detail, including its economic rise, sports stories, changes led by women, media and Bollywood, bureaucratic ventures and so on. After all, there were daily feeds coming in from journalists like Preeti Dahiya and Jyoti Yadav; Miss World Manushi Chillar was taking the world by storm, with every Instagram post. Then there were regular stories from farmers from different parts of Haryana converging towards Delhi borders for the protest which had become more political than ever before. In contrast, there were stories of sportstars like Ravi Kumar Dahiya, Sushil Kumar, Bajrang Poonia, Sarita Mor, Vinesh Phogat, among many others. And, Neeraj Chopra!

I was on my terrace managing college teaching, immersed in the work of the first book and looking for opportunities when one fine day, editor and friend, Yamini, asked me if I would be interested in writing about Neeraj Chopra. I remember getting up from my table and going to my wife.

'You think I should do it?'

'Arjun, you are a better judge. Do what your heart says.'

And, so was it. With publishers sorted, I began researching on the story of sports in Haryana and the star of the day, Neeraj Chopra.

Neeraj by then had become a national star. I was living in Panipat then. And I would know from newspapers when Neeraj was in town. He would meet people, fans would throng to get pictures clicked and Neeraj would always be seen smiling. I thought to myself, '*Ab to aadat ho gayi hogi*' (It must be a habit by now). It had been close to a month since Neeraj had made history by winning the first gold medal at athletics in the Olympics. In the process, he was the only second Indian after shooter Abhinav Bindra to win an individual gold. India's performance in so many Olympics prior had been dismal to say the least. The only silver lining was the hockey glory and some other individual efforts. For a nation which had only recently started to look beyond cricket, Neeraj brought big smiles and bigger aspirations.

Cricket has been an obsession in the country. And there is big money involved! Many fans stay glued to the game, seldom venturing out to other sports. As a consequence, other sports suffer and so do the players who are probably giving it all that they have to improve the situation they are in.

Hence, when Neeraj won gold at the Games, I was ecstatic. I remember telling myself, '*Lathh gadd diya chhore ne* (He has proven his mettle).' After all it was no small feat. One, it was the Olympic Games which brings together the best contingents on the planet, and secondly where he had come from. It's not just the success but also the journey to it which makes it stand out amongst all. These, though, my initial impressions, were good enough to motivate me to explore the subject further.

'*Ab karein kya?* (What to do now?)'

For all fresh and ambitious writers, it is a great thing to have an idea but then there is a process to develop it. Every writer has their own process. I began with mine. I started reading articles and watching innumerable interviews that had flooded the internet. Instagram, particularly, was flooded with his bytes. The platform has made remarkable inroads into the lives of Haryanvis and young Indians. I found so many of these videos with a background score that could be great gym music only if they were longer than 15 seconds.

But in order to get Neeraj's story, I had to connect the dots unheard of in the media—away from the limelight. I reached out to Shagun. He is a humble and dedicated local reporter from Haryana working for the Hindi daily, *Aaj Samaj*. His support had been paramount in numerous initiatives we took at the Rath Foundation, which had taken up many projects in sectors like education, empowerment and environment (what I call the three Es of social development). Connected to me through the school teachers at my mother's workplace, Shagun has been doing good reporting in Panipat despite being curtailed twice a week due to his kidney ailment. I asked him, 'Do you know Neeraj Chopra or anyone close to him?'

'Kamaal kar di, Bauji. Aise logon se milaaunga jinhone usse haath mein thamaayi hai javelin (Obviously, Sir. I will introduce you to people who have put javelin in his hand).'

I recollect thinking, *'Bhai, bhaavanaaon mein beh gaya'* (Brother became over-sentimental). But well, I did not have many places to start with. And so, I started by telling him that I wanted to write something about Neeraj and needed his help. *'Don't worry, Bauji. Aap yeh bataao Panipat next kab aaoge'* (Don't worry, Sir. Just let me know when will you be in Panipat next).

I had been travelling all over for my work. Delhi, Narnaul, Mussoorie, Rohtak, Panchkula, Hisar and so on—it became never-ending at a point. So much so that I was averaging 400 km a day in a car for two weeks straight! Hence, when I reached Panipat, I was not particularly keen on driving where Shagun had called me.

From where I stay in Panipat to the old residential part of the city, Model Town, it is a drive through bad traffic snarls. But we do what we have to do, right? I started from GT Road, to Assandh Road and then took a left for Ram Lal Chowk. Further down, I took a right to get onto the

Ring Road of Panipat and reached a sports store.

This was the first time I had met Shagun in person. From his pictures he looked like a bright young man. I, of course, knew about his ailment, but never expected him to have lost so much weight. But the energy and life you see in him is remarkable. Ever eager, ever ready, ever smiling.

We met at Brand Hut store. The owner of the store is a young Sikh entrepreneur who runs sportswear stores, a sports goods factory and other small ventures. It is not tough to understand that this man loves javelin for there were two in an otherwise clothing and shoe store. The man I met was Sunny. Now, even when I write this, I have to look through my notes to remember what his actual name is. Be it the stadium or neighbourhood, this man, who was once a young and promising javelin thrower, is called by just one name.

Sunny is a humble man who had risen from limited means. Self-respecting and happy-go-lucky, Sunny's pictures from his youth show how slim and fit he was, in contrast to who I met. Sunny started telling his story. With some drinks and the company of other players in the store, we began discussing sports in Haryana and Neeraj Chopra.

By this point, I had started making notes of Neeraj's journey. I had briefs about his journey through news reports, interviews etc., but those details were rather incomplete. He had already been a star—the first Indian to bag a medal at the Olympics in athletics, and that too a gold! It was bound to take him to stardom. And all that stardom was accompanied by money, fame, limelight, media glare and connections.

Neeraj by then was just everywhere. A #neerajchopra search could lead me to innumerable posts credited to him. But that was not just it. Neeraj's story was waiting to be told. This interest developed into a strange resolve after I met Sunny. He helped connect it all. And that is how I went finding Neeraj's friends, colleagues, family and so on.

I remember one subject telling me, *'Sir, iss poore process mein sabse zyada mazaa aapko aane waalaa hai'* (Sir, you will be the one enjoying the most in this entire process). It was at the Brand Hut store of Sunny while I was discussing with a group of current and former sportsmen of Shivaji Stadium—and indeed that was the case—when I began enjoying the process so much that I became ready to meet any person who would tell me Neeraj's story. Be it early morning or late at night!

I have to agree that the bigger motivation was Haryana. The state was already a sports powerhouse and understanding what was bringing this change was a great motivation in itself. From Sunny to Kashinath Naik, I ended up speaking to innumerable people about Neeraj and a common theme prevailed—Neeraj was such a grounded person that it was a delight meeting him. And that is what I felt when I met him.

Neeraj is a star. He is rich and famous, he attracts fans in millions. He is the best face for brand endorsements today. Yet, when I met him, he came across as an extremely humble and cheerful person, with absolutely no airs about what he has achieved. He is definitely aware of how big of a thing he has achieved, but is ready to share his story very honestly. And when in presence of his uncles, his poise is a little reserved out of respect for the seniors.

He is not out of reach for people who have been part of his journey. With so much going on in his life, certain people might think that he is no longer available, but that is not the case. It is his grounded nature that has perfected his smiling pose. He is trying hard to accommodate everyone's wishes. He speaks to all guests, attends programmes, does brand endorsements and lives a full life in the process.

∽

The book begins with his Tokyo qualifiers. However, from thereon it traces his journey back. It discusses the state of Haryana and javelin as a sport as well. For instance, there was Anglo-Indian Elizabeth Davenport who won medals at the Asian Games (1958 and 1962). Then it was Razia Sheikh who broke Davenport's 21-year-old record in 1986. She went a step further becoming the first Indian woman to cross the 50-m barrier at the 1987 South Asian Games in Kolkata.

Similarly, there was Anil Kumar from Haryana who broke a decade-old record in 2008 and in the process became the first Indian player to cross the 80-m barrier in men's javelin throw in Bhopal.[1] And there are also stories of Neeraj's friends and seniors who gave him early lessons in the game. The book also takes the reader from Shivaji Stadium in Panipat to Panchkula and then to the national camp in Patiala. The National Institute of Sports (NIS), Patiala, or more precisely the Netaji Subhash National Institute of Sports, was founded in 1961. NIS was later merged with the Sports Authority of India (SAI) and is housed in the Moti Bagh Palace of the erstwhile royal family of Patiala.

The book also takes the reader through the challenges of a sportsperson's life and covers Neeraj's journey in the right stead. Of course, there is more to him than what the book has explored and his path ahead is clear. There are more competitions and medals to win, but for now his Olympic glory is the zenith for sportspersons in India dreaming of winning a gold medal at the Olympics.

---

[1]'Singh's Indian Javelin Throw record the highlight in Bhopal', *World Athletics*, 19 September 2008, https://worldathletics.org/news/news/singhs-indian-javelin-throw-record-the-highli. Accessed on 29 November 2021.

1

2020 Tokyo Olympics

The Japanese prefecture was ready for the Olympics that began on 23 July 2021. The nation's mood was set after the COVID-19 crisis had already delayed the mega-event for a year. When the Rio Olympics took place in 2016, the world had no idea that a pandemic would impact humanity to the extent that time would virtually come to a standstill. Colloquially! The land of the rising sun was finally ready to host the Olympics since 2013 when the nation had first bid for it.

Owing to the pandemic, the Games, otherwise scheduled for July–August 2020, took place a year later. They opened on 23 July 2021 and closed on 8 August 2021. And the motto for the Games reflected perfectly what the world had been going through: 'United by Emotion'.

The Olympics, officially called the Games of the XXXII Olympiad, was the most significant international multi-sport event that brought together 206 nations. More than 11,500 athletes participated in 339 events. Such a gathering of peak human endurance coming together in a city was a clear example of what humankind could achieve. However, unlike other times, the Games were largely held behind closed doors due to the pandemic. The main stadium for the event was the former National Stadium, the central venue for the 1964 Summer Olympics. But this also was not free of all troubles.

After Japan submitted its bid to host the Olympics, murmurs of either renovating or reconstructing the National Stadium started making rounds. The premises would host the opening and closing ceremonies along with track and field events. Early in 2012, they decided that the stadium would be demolished and reconstructed. To do that, the government contracted a reputed British Iraqi architect, Zaha Hadid. Hadid offered some bold designs and submitted the renderings late in 2012. It was hoped that with all permissions and contracts in place the venue would be ready for 2019 Rugby World Cup.

However, many Japanese designers criticized Hadid, the first woman to win the Pritzker Architecture Prize in 2004. *The Guardian* in November 2014 read: 'It was supposed to represent a dynamic future vision for Tokyo, flaring up out of the city's Meiji Jingu Park in sinuous white arcs. But Zaha Hadid's design for the 2020 Olympic stadium has been subjected to a two-year tirade of criticism, alterations and budget cuts—and it is now facing its fiercest public attack yet.[1] Even after revisions following budget cuts, someone called it a monumental mistake and somebody said that it would look like a gigantic bicycle helmet plopped down in the gardens.[2] There were still others who compared it to a turtle and even an elephant.[3] Amidst all the criticism, revisions and budget cuts, the project was majorly re-done. The retractable roof was out of the plan and a change in seating led to the current stadium taking shape. This, however, meant that the stadium would not be ready in time for the Rugby World cup.

In June 2015, the Japanese government reached a new agreement to construct the main venue for the 2020 Olympics and Paralympics.[4] They scrapped a few innovative things as the prices skyrocketed. But with timely execution, the new National Stadium, which would oversee

---

[1] Wainwright, Oliver. 'Zaha Hadid's Tokyo Olympic stadium slammed as a "monumental mistake" and "disgrace to future generations"', *The Guardian*, 6 November 2014, https://www.theguardian.com/artanddesign/architecture-design-blog/2014/nov/06/zaha-hadids-tokyo-olympic-stadium-slammed-as-a-monumental-mistake-and-a-disgrace-to-future-generations. Accessed on 29 November 2021.
[2] Ibid.
[3] 'New National, Maintenance Cost 250 Billion Yen Settled by Maintaining the Conventional Design', Nikkei, 24 June 2015, https://www.nikkei.com/article/DGXLASDG23H9L_T20C15A6EA2000/. Accessed on 29 November 2021.
[4] Ibid.

the fortunes of many, was ready in time for the Olympics and inaugurated on 21 December 2019.[5] A notable feature of the stadium premises was that they used timber as a significant component, sourced from all 47 prefectures of Japan following the tradition set by the Meiji Shrine. The shrine, built in remembrance of Emperor Meiji and his wife Empress Shoken, has around 120,000 trees donated by people from all parts of Japan.

Pandemic Hits

However, just across the waters, another storm was brewing. In December 2019, the coronavirus spread in Wuhan, China, and took the world by storm. It impacted every country on the planet with severe fatality rates. Japan was no different. Japan's national capital, Tokyo, which had hosted similar events and is among the most progressive cities globally, was caught in the conundrum.

The Olympic Games are the most expensive sporting events and this one surpassed all previous financial benchmarks. Many investments had gone by in the last many years to prepare this wonderful city for the Games. But, as the pandemic continued its aggression unabated, it was time to take a firm decision.

---

[5]Bernardi, Par Kevin. 'Inauguration Officielle du Stade Olympique', 22 December 2019, https://sportetsociete.org/2019/12/22/tokyo-2020-inauguration-officielle-du-stade-olympique/. Accessed on 29 November 2021.

In March 2020, when the pandemic was still in its early stages, different countries had started speculating that the Games could be cancelled or postponed. Cancelling the Games was a long shot since it had only happened during times of war. The previous Games in Rio were held when the Zika virus was still round the corner. Hence, the question of a cancellation did not even arise. Japan, like many other nations and international organizations, was monitoring the situation very closely.[6]

However, owing to the global concerns around public health and safety, the president of the International Olympic committee (IOC) and prime minister of Japan, Shinzo Abe, held a conference call with members of the organizing committee and others. On 24 March 2020, the committee issued a joint statement:

> The unprecedented and unpredictable spread of the outbreak has seen the situation in the rest of the world deteriorating. Yesterday, the Director-General of the World Health Organisation (WHO), Tedros Adhanom Ghebreyesus, said the COVID-19 pandemic is 'accelerating'. There are more than 375,000 cases now recorded worldwide, and in nearly every country,

---

[6]Trotter, Anthony and Winsor, Morgan. 'No Plans to Cancel or Postpone Tokyo 2020 Olympics Amid Coronavirus Outbreak', abcNews, 2 March 2020, https://abcnews.go.com/International/plans-cancel-postpone-tokyo-2020-olympics-amid-coronavirus/story?id=69281972. Accessed on 29 November 2021.

their numbers are growing by the hour. In the present circumstances and based on the information provided by the WHO today, the IOC President and the Prime Minister of Japan have concluded that the Games of the XXXII Olympiad in Tokyo must be rescheduled to a date beyond 2020 but not later than summer 2021, to safeguard the health of the athletes, everybody involved in the Olympic Games and the international community.

The leaders agreed that the Olympic Games in Tokyo could stand as a beacon of hope to the world during these troubled times, and the Olympic flame could become the light at the end of the tunnel in which the world finds itself at present. They also agreed that the Olympic flame would stay in Japan and would keep the name—Tokyo 2020 Olympics And Paralympics. Hence, the leaders moved the Games to July–August 2021.

In between this gap of months, the world saw millions of lives lost to the pandemic. By mid-2021, the situation started to improve. Although the fears were still looming large, the economic costs, athlete preparations, TV rights etc., made compelling reasons for the Games to be held now. Hence, with the venue and schedule set, the world was ready for to witness human's inhuman resolve, strength and conviction to surpass physical and mental performance limits.

Javelin in Olympics

Athletic events constitute the largest group of events at the Olympics. It consists of track and field in addition to the road events and Decathlon, among others. The track and field events at Tokyo 2020 began at the new Olympic stadium, which was a fine setting for the biggest spectacle. Track events are mostly racing events. The area inside the track and around it was used for field events such as high jump, pole vault, long jump, triple jump, discus throw, hammer throw, shot-put throw and javelin throw runways.[7]

Usually, in field events, each player takes turns at performance-setting benchmarks for the competitors. Top athletes from each nation first take part in the qualification rounds. Athletes who qualify for the finals perform and outperform in the final events. Javelin throw was added to the men's programme at London in 1908. Since then, that has remained unchanged. Incidentally, Javelin throw is the only throwing performance at the Games, preceded by an approach run.

At the Tokyo Olympics, athletics events started on 30 July and javelin events began on 3 August, with the Women's Javelin Throw qualification—Group A event. Men's Javelin Throw qualifications began on 4 August. Two young men represented India—23-year-old Neeraj Chopra and 26-year-

---

[7]Olympics, Tokyo 2020, https://olympics.com/en/olympic-games/tokyo-2020. Accessed on 29 November 2021.

old Shivpal Singh. The latter came with a solid legacy of javelin—his father, uncles and brothers were all throwers.[8] Chandauli (Uttar Pradesh) resident Shivpal, who is currently serving in the Indian Air Force, threw his personal best of 86.23 m at the 2019 Asian Championships in Doha.[9]

It was, however, Shivpal's 85.47 m throw in his fifth attempt at the Athletics Central North West (ACNW) League, a pre-season meet at the Kenneth McArthur Stadium, in Potchefstroom, South Africa, in March 2020 that ensured his qualification for Tokyo. Chopra also had qualified for the Olympics at the ACNW League meeting, with a throw of 87.86 m. This was considerably farther than the qualification mark of 85 m. The Athletics Federation of India (AFI) confirmed the validity of the competition and the two players were set for the Men's Javelin Throw at Tokyo 2020. Annu Rani from Meerut, UP, represented the Women's Javelin team.

∽

The country sent its largest contingent of 126 players for the Olympics. As the Games opened, the anticipation was

---

[8]Gupta, Uday. 'Tokyo 2020: Javelin Star Shivpal Singh Ready to Make India Proud at Upcoming Olympic Games', 13 July 2021, https://www.indiatoday.in/sports/tokyo-olympics/story/javelin-star-shivpal-singh-ready-to-make-india-proud-at-tokyo-2020-1827501-2021-07-13. Accessed on 29 November 2021.

[9]Singh, Shivpal. *World Athletics*, https://worldathletics.org/athletes/india/shivpal-singh-14722564. Acessed on 29 November 2021.

high. More than a few Indians were now medal hopefuls. Boxer Mary Kom and field hockey captain Manpreet Singh were the flag bearers of the Indian contingent at the opening ceremony.

Wednesday, 4 August 2021, 9 a.m.: The day was bright with stray clouds breaching a clear sky. At 32°C and 69 per cent humidity, the field was set for the Men's Javelin Throw qualification round. A total of 32 players were divided into two groups: A and B. The qualifying mark was 83.50 m, which meant that at least 12 best performers would advance to the final.

The Group A contest began at 9.08 a.m. with Alexandru Mihaita Novac flinging his javelin to 83.27 m in his first attempt. Neeraj Chopra was fifteenth on the list. It was a very big day for family, friends, seniors and a long list of coaches and supporters in India. Indeed, for well-wishers of Indian athletics, India had not been a very successful nation at athletics in Olympics. And Neeraj Chopra had become a medal prospect already. He had recovered from his elbow injury and was making his dominating presence felt in the season already.

The broadcasting agency showed the fine details of the 16 athletes on television screens. But the fine print lay in the season's best. Germany's Johannes Vetter, who has been a dominating force in the sport, did a season's best of 96.29 m while his personal best was 97.76 m. Neeraj was only second to him in the season's best performance of 88.07 m. He entered the competition at an exceptional performance stage. This was, of course, reflected in his throw.

Vetter, with an exceptional personal best could throw 82.04 m in his first throw, only qualifying in this third attempt with 85.64 m. Finnish Lassi Etelätalo threw 84.50 m qualifying in his first attempt.

Neeraj Chopra came up, wearing a dark blue sports vest, bib number 2297, with a headband to keep his hair in control. He adjusted his lower back brace, stretched and settled it, shook his left leg and knee. Adjusting his right hand to the grip on the 800 g implement, he stretched his shoulder and lifted the spear just the right amount above his head. Taking long, high strides in white shoes and stretch pants, he ran with high raised knees towards the throwing arc. With adequate pace in order, he began turning his body sideways, started running with side steps—a very focused run-up! He extended his right arm all the way back, stretching the full shoulder and made the cross over. In a split second with full might and roar, the javelin speared high into the sky and Neeraj landed on his hands, ensuring he did not cross the throwing arc.[10]

In his first attempt at the Olympics, Neeraj had topped the Round A charts with a sensational throw of 86.65 m. He had cleared the qualifying mark by over three metres! He knew it was a good throw. He casually turned around,

---

[10]Neeraj CHOPRA, *International Olympic Committee*, https://olympics.com/en/athletes/neeraj-chopra. Accessed on 30 November 2021.

strolled towards the bench like a regular day, lifted his blue jacket and walked back. It was a drill he had practised on numerous occasions earlier. His yellow javelin throw had done the day's job. Neeraj had entered the finals.

However, in Group B, Shivpal Singh who had trained under German coach Uwe Hohn and attended training programmes in South Africa was not that lucky. In the three attempts, he made a best effort of 76.40 m and failed to qualify.[11] India's medal prospects in athletics were now solely on the athletic shoulders of this 23-year-old from Panipat, Haryana.

History of Javelin

Javelin throwing has ancient roots. Cave paintings worldwide depict early Homo sapiens throwing spears to bring down an animal for safety or even for food. This spear skill has only developed alongside as the human civilization progressed in science and technology. Different civilization such as Persians, Indians and the Greco-Romans all have extensive religious, military, sports traditions and rituals linked to the spear. For instance, the Battle of Hydaspes River in which Porus fought Alexander describes weaponry thus:

---

[11]'India's Neeraj Chopra Eases into Tokyo Olympics Javelin Final, Shivpal Bows Out', *International Olympic Committee*, https://olympics.com/en/news/tokyo-olympics-javelin-throw-qualification-neeraj-chopra-shivpal-singh-result. Accessed on 1 December 2021.

'The more dignified Indians use sunshades against the summer heat. They have slippers of white skin, and these too made neatly; and the soles of their sandals are of different colours and also high, so that the wearers seem taller. Indian war equipment differs; the infantry has a bow, of the height of the owner. This they poise on the ground, and set their left foot against it, and shoot thus: drawing the bowstring a very long way back, for their arrows are little short of three cubits. Nothing can stand against an arrow shot by an Indian archer, neither shield nor breastplate nor any strong armour. In their left hand they carry small shields of untanned hide, narrower than their bearers, but not much shorter. Some have javelins in place of bows. All carry a broad scimitar, its length not under three cubits; and this, when they have a hand-to-hand fight—and Indians do not readily fight so among themselves—they bring down with both hands in smiting, so that the stroke may be an effective one. Their horsemen have two javelins, like lances, and a small shield smaller than the infantry's. The horses have no saddles, nor do they use Greek bits nor any like the Celtic bits, but round the end of the horses' mouths they have an untanned stitched rein fitted. In this they have fitted, on the inner side, bronze or iron spikes, but rather blunted; the rich people have ivory spikes. Within the mouth of the horses is a bit, like a spit, to either end of which the reins are attached. Then when they tighten the reins this bit masters the horse, and the spikes, being attached thereto, prick the horse and compel it to obey the rein.'[12]

Whilst the modern understanding of the sport of javelin originated with the Greek Olympics, there is evidence of spear throwing elsewhere too. Like the Tamil Sangam Literature dated around the second century discusses in detail the martial training with various weapons, particularly a Vel, or spear, and how recruits would specialize and compete with one another. Hence, both martial and competitive sporting nature were clubbed together.

At the ancient Olympics, the sport was a part of the Pentathlon. The Pentathlon was a five-event game played for the first time in the Olympics of 708 BC that included javelin throw, running, wrestling, discus throw and jumping. The event had two forms of the javelin event, one measuring distance thrown and another to hit a specific target.

The 1908 Olympics witnessed the first Men's Javelin event while the 1932 event added the Women's Javelin discipline. Brothers Bud and Dick from the US designed the modern-day javelin in the 1950s. They constructed a longer, slimmer implement, hollow in the centre with more surface area. As the sport evolved so did the javelin with new materials and different weight requirements. Players practised with different implements, including ones made out of bamboo.

---

[12]Arrian. *Annabis Alexandri Book VIII (Indica)*, Google Books.

Known as World Athletics (since 2019), it was formed in the 1912 Olympics by the International Amateur Athletic Federation (IAAF), which regulates athletics. The organization sets the rules and regulations for this sport, in particular the design of the javelin and record-keeping.

Better conditioning, training and other advances saw the sport develop and world records were shattered continuously, culminating in a world record distance set by German athlete Uwe Hohn in 1984. Hohn was born in 1962 and started competing and excelling in the sport at a young age. In 1984, he threw the longest Javelin throw ever at 104.80 m.[13] To date, he is the only one to have crossed the 100-m barrier. Further, the record he established stays till perpetuity since the new javelin design was implemented from 1986.

Long throw distances, such as these, posed significant safety risks as there was the possibility of overshooting the stadium and the javelin landing in the crowd. Further, the earlier design of the javelin made flat landings more frequent. As a consequence, the javelin was redesigned and record-keeping started all over. Its centre of gravity was moved forward; the surface area in front of that centre was reduced while the surface area behind it was increased. This ensured that the javelin stuck into the ground more consistently.

---

[13]'Uwe Hohn German Athlete', *Britannica*, https://www.britannica.com/biography/Uwe-Hohn. Accessed on 1 December 2021.

The modern-day javelin is made from metal or carbon fibre, ending in a metal spear-like point, but it no longer has the leather thong like it did in ancient Greece. Various track-and-field or javelin-throwing associations and clubs exist on the local-to-international level as well, in which men and women alike compete. Among others, two important competing categories are the U-20/Junior and Senior. In both these, the weight of the javelins is the same—800 g for men and 600 g for women.

∽

Javelin in Haryana

Javelin throwing was not an all-time popular sport in Haryana. However, owing to a culture of toil, players would play the sport. In the early days, the town of Bhiwani became a sporting hub for javelin throwers. This was followed by Hisar and then the entire region. However, there is no particular pattern as to where the sport became particularly popular.

One needs to understand it thus: boys and girls don't just one day decide to choose a sport. There are various factors that come into play before one decided which sport to pursue. Significant factors that came into play were inspiration and available facilities.

If a specific player or coach brought laurels to a certain sport, people and consequently their young ones are inspired to pursue it. This also meant that facilities around this player/coaches' vicinity would surely be better than elsewhere.

A fair example was the Neeraj Impact, a report suggested that owing to Neeraj's success, Panipat stadium saw as many as 60 fresh entrants daily. Over 25 javelins were being sold everyday at sportstores in the vicinity.[14] When I visited the Shivaji Stadium on multiple occasions, I saw Neeraj's poster hanging there, passively nudging many. A javelin thrower, Sunny gleefully remarked, '*Bahaut bachche aa gaye hain ji ab javelin khelne*' (Many children have arrived to play with the javelin).

---

[14]Mishra, Ashutosh. 'Neeraj Chopra impact: Tokyo 2020 gold inspires young athletes to take up javelin in Olympic champion's village', *India Today*, https://www.indiatoday.in/sports/tokyo-olympics/story/be-like-neeraj-chopra-tokyo-2020-gold-inspires-more-panipat-kids-to-take-up-javelin-1838986-2021-08-10. Accessed on 10 December 2021.

2

Haryana and History

'Jiddi Haryana'

—Neeraj Chopra

The land on the three sides of Delhi; jutting Punjab and Rajasthan and skirting the Yamuna River on one side is the state of Haryana. The word 'Haryana' means 'Land of the Gods' or the 'Abode of Hari'. There are other epithets given to the name of the state such as 'Green Forest'. There are still older names such as 'Bahudhanyaka' (land of abundance) and 'Dharamkshetra Kurukshetra' related to the region. However, all these names suggested a common understanding that this region was once a flourishing central node of the Indic civilization.

It was on the banks of the Saraswati River, which flowed through the region, where the vedas were written. The greatest battle between good and evil—the Mahabharata—was fought on the banks of the same river. Lord Krishna delivered his sermon 'Gita Saar', which has guided the Hindu community for millennia in Jyotisar, Kurukshetra; this is a clear testimony of Haryana's glory.

However, by the break of the last millennia, Haryana had become a battleground of civilizations. This began early during the medieval ages when Haryana became a pit stop en route to Delhi and further into India for the Islamic invaders. Sirsa, Fatehabad and Hisar from one side and Ambala, Karnal and Panipat, on the other, became significant conflict zones. At Taraori, King Prithviraj Chauhan defeated Mohammad Ghori in AD 1191. The Sultanate kings also used this region for their numerous conflicts. Feroze Shah Tughlaq built the prosperous towns of Hisar. Still, Hansi and Agroha continued to be the crucial centres of trade and commerce.

North of Delhi, in modern Haryana, is the town of Karnal that saw significant battles in Taraori, Kunjpura, etc. Even the great sack of Mughal Delhi by Persian Nadir Shah began with the battle of Karnal. Then, of course, there is the famed town of Panipat.

Panipat lies about 100 km north of modern-day Khan Market, Delhi. In the medieval ages, it had been a front and battleground of three big wars which divide epochs between them—AD 1526, 1556 and 1761. But before we delve into that, let us understand some history and physiological aspects that brought to us this glory.

～

The discussion on Indian male physiology is essential. During ancient India, Bharat was both culturally and economically strong. The wealth generated provided a lifestyle and standard of living that most European observers would either be dismissive of or not achieve till the Renaissance. Hence, there was enough food to eat, decent medical facilities and a strong governance support system. An obvious by-product of the same is the strong physiology of the residents here. An example of this could be the description of Raja Porus.

Porus was a ruler of a fiefdom and clashed with Alexander the Great at the Battle of Hydaspes River—the Jhelum River located in modern-day Punjab. The Greek historian Plutarch writes in *The Life of Alexander* with detail on the campaign against Raja Porus. However, what is fascinating is the description of Raja Porus as a massive king who stood seven feet tall, an exceptional warrior and greatly skilled at riding an elephant.

Whilst this is one example of one individual, the data available from the medieval period describing the people who inhabited this area indicates a difference in physiology. Arrian, the Macedonian chronicler for Alexander the Great, described the following 'All the territory that lies west of the river Indus up to the River Cophen [River Kabul] is inhabited by Astacenians and Assacenians, Indian tribes. But they are not, like the Indians dwelling within the river Indus, tall of stature, nor similarly brave in spirit, nor as black as the greater part of the Indians.'[15]

Similarly, Fa-Hein in his travels to India wrote the following with respect to public philanthropy benefactors endowing hospitals for the poor, widowers, and cripples: 'They are well taken care of under and attending physicians are given their prescribed food and medicine only discharged when they are cured.'[16] The abundance of food and the ability to stave off famine for prolonged periods supported the physiological development that allowed life expectancy to be sustainable and medical knowledge to grow alongside it.

However, the nation entered the dark ages in its medieval era. Apart from conversions and battles, the region suffered from innumerable atrocities. The East India Company's rule followed in India, after which came the British Empire. For centuries, the country faced knowledge loss, economic onslaught and famines, leading to utter disaster for the Indian strength.

The fatality figures, for instance, are horrifying from 1770 to 1900. Some 25 million Indians supposedly died

---

[15] Arrian, *Anabasis Alexandri Book VIII*, Kessinger Publishing Co, 2004.
[16] Beal, Samuel. *Travels of Fah-Hian and Sung-Yun, Buddhist Pilgrims, from China to India (400 A.D. and 518 A.D.)*, The classics. Us, 2013.

in famines, including 15 million in the five famines in the second half of the nineteenth century. The famines of the twentieth century probably took the total well over 35 million.[17]

But that may be just one part of India because while this was happening, there is still evidence of glorious ages in other parts of India, particularly in the South and the East.

∽

The Indian male physiology hence has a story of a deep dive and a swift rise post-Independence. India fought through a grain crisis, and incorporated better living standards and eating habits with economic reforms. Considering the famines and their aftermath, India's rise in sporting glory has been remarkable. Of course, this needs a much more detailed analysis by researchers. But this provides an excellent start to understanding how Haryanvis made this region a sporting powerhouse.

For the longest time, the region of Haryana has suffered onslaughts to preserve Delhi. After the decline of the Saraswati-Sindhu civilization, the Mahabharata was fought here. These lands and the ones extending further to the west also bore the brunt of the Islamic conquests. There were battles here and villages in the region that had to naturally face the repercussions of the anarchy that spread all across.

---

[17]Tharoor, Shashi. *An Era of Darkness: The British Empire in India*, Aleph Book Company, 2016, p. 162.

Furthermore, Haryana, after the decline of the Saraswati drainage system, became semi-arid in the arid region. In fact, as recently as six decades ago, the outskirts of Hisar were sandy. There were small dunes, and dust storms were not very uncommon. I remember sitting amongst a group of senior professionals—doctors, academics and retired air force officers—at Savant Hospital in Hisar who could easily recollect those days. A lot has changed since then.

∽

'*Kuchh tha hi nahin* (there was nothing here)'—was the oft-repeated phrase I heard as I spoke with R.K. Sangwan, a swimmer, who recollected those days when I attempted to dig out the story of Haryana's sports after Independence.

Haryana had suffered most during the Islamic invasion, the East India Company rule and the British reign. They assured that the Punjab region flourished and Haryana suffered, acting as a buffer zone. This tragedy continued post-Independence when the Ambala Division (Haryana today) of joint Punjab continued with the step-brotherly treatment of the region.

There were no avenues and no opportunities for Haryanvis in sports during those days. This, however, does not mean that sports was not appreciated or supported by locals. What it does mean is that the future in sports for young boys and girls was not bright. And why was that? Because there were limited avenues and opportunities.

Former bureaucrat and a shining personality, Yudhbir Singh Khyalia, whose hearty laughter could wake up anybody's inner child with love shared that sports were in the genes. Villagers would sing praises of sporting glories at the local level. Gossip of *chusti-furti* in kabaddi or kushti (wrestling) was always talked about and appreciated.

The septuagenarian recollected how the tug of war team of their village won a competition in Lahore, when he was a young boy. The village welcomed the team with much fanfare. The rewards then were cans of ghee and a token sum of money. That also brings us to the eternal love of Haryanvi diet—ghee. It was and is just everything. A solution to all problems, food for all ailments, nutrition for the biggest glories.

Ghee cans used to be given or gifted to big sports stars in the region. Hence, one could imagine the economic aspect behind this. Money, cars and laurels are modern gifts. For a society that was parched, receiving a can of ghee was the ultimate honour. And that is was Sangwan meant.

Further, there were no means to improve skills and nurture talent. He is in awe of what he sees today in comparison to his days. For instance, Sangwan learnt to swim after his father threw him into the Johad village pond that was used for water conservation and mostly as a shared bath for buffaloes and cattle. He remembered his father giving him a *matka* (earthen pot) to hold to save him from drowning. He then started flapping his legs to learn to swim. This was followed by holding onto a buffalo's tail.

Such are the tales of limited means and avenues that Haryana was going through. *Par bataye kaun?* (But who would bell the cat?) These stories are mostly lost and seem a little too difficult to believe. But they all are real!

∾

However, there was always the spirit and drive to excel. Be better and the best at whatever one was doing. Haryanvis have always been highly driven and strong-willed people. Pinch their egos, and they end up shaking the world around them in response. But this strong will found very few avenues in those days.

I remember sitting in the living room of a house in Mayfair Garden, Hauz Khas, of a mentor and previous boss. In a conversation about Haryana, someone made quite an insightful remark: 'You see, they are remarkable people. An amazing lot. They have a strange drive; you give them whichever field to excel in, and they will. The community needs to be provided direction, and the entire lot will go in that direction and conquer it. Look at sports, civil services or even entrepreneurship.'

The remark made in jest made complete sense to the audience and everyone nodded in apparent understanding. The comment was more on Jats in the region, but it held true for the entire territory. That is Haryana! And such are Haryanvis!

Another driving factor has been the military tradition

of the region. Haryana has been a recruitment centre of forces for the longest time now. The hard-rugged men of the region have for over two decades in the modern military tradition served in the services. These men would get exposed to the contemporary ways of the world.

The military also has a long-standing tradition of sports. Hence, when the retirees came back they would continue playing and consequently inspire the next generation. The Haryanvis are a sporting state can be understood from the fact that it is easy to find young boys and girls running on roads and fields every morning in villages and outside. I have witnessed this beautiful sight on innumerable occasions driving across the region while attempting to understand the state.

These young people are the future. They are the reflection of the society that the region wants to build. It is aspirational and ambitious. It is not afraid to give all of themselves a way grander goal than their village chaupal. So, a story of a boy from Khandra who made history in Tokyo is inspiring and touches the right chords of every boy or girl looking forward to achieve their dream.

∽

Sporting stars such as Lila Ram Sangwan and Hawa Singh also came from Haryana back in the day. Hawa Singh was born in Bhiwani in December 1937 and was recruited by the Army when he was 19. He became a two-time Asian gold medallist and remained national boxing champion for 11 consecutive years. He represented the beginning of Bhiwani's boxing glory. In 1986, when the SAI centre opened its doors, two players began training under Singh. Over the years, the number has grown multifold.[18]

Similarly, Sangwan was a prominent wrestler who represented India at the 1956 Olympics. Lila Ram was the first Indian wrestler to win the gold at the Commonwealth Games in 1958. Fighting heavyweight, he defeated Jacobus Hanekom to win the gold. But a policy change in Haryana provided a specific push to sporting history in the region.

On 15 January 2001, *The Tribune* wrote: 'Punjab, which once used to be the leading state in sport in India, has now taken a backseat. In Haryana, it is perhaps the political will that has helped sports to grow. It is only in school sport that Punjab is ahead of Haryana.[19]

At the break of the century, Karnam Malleswari became the first female weightlifter to win a medal at the Sydney Olympics. The Haryana government announced ₹25 lakh for her for bringing in the bronze medal. Malleswari was married into a Yamunanagar family. When she won the

---

[18]Deswal, Deepender. 'Bhiwani Boxing Legend Hawa Singh to Come Alive on Silver Screen', *The Tribune*, 4 February 2020, https://www.tribuneindia.com/news/haryana/bhiwani-boxing-legend-hawa-singh-to-come-alive-on-silver-screen-36001. Accessed on 29 November 2021.

[19]Katyal, Arvind . 'Punjab Can Learn from Haryana', *Chandigarh Tribune*, 15 January 2001, https://www.tribuneindia.com/2001/20010115/cth3.htm. Accessed on 29 November 2021.

medal, O.P. Chautala phoned her in Sydney and promised land and a house to set up an academy. This set a precedent and in the following years, the Haryana government's interest in sports only grew.

In the last two decades, chief ministers Bhupinder Singh Hooda and then Manohar Lal Khattar have increased the reward money for sportsperson and provided them with all sorts of perks. A September 2014 *Hindustan Times* article described it thus: 'Huge cash rewards, jobs in the police and other departments, luxury cars like Audis and SX-4s, smartphones, land for sports academies, stadiums for villages of sportspersons and hundreds of kilograms of desi ghee, or clarified butter, Hooda has certainly pampered Haryana's achiever sportspersons with goodies. The results are there for all to see. Between 25 to 30 per cent of all medal-winning sportspersons for the country in the Olympics, Asian Games and Commonwealth Games have a Haryana connection.[20]

The Hooda government ensured that the sportspersons received incentives such as cash rewards, jobs and honours. Sportspersons who excelled received more than ₹82 crore as rewards and many of them were appointed to government jobs—from DSPs to other positions. In 10 years of his tenure, the Haryana government also built 15

---

[20]IANS. 'Hooda is undisputed king of Haryana's sports', *Hindustan Times*, 3 September 2014, https://www.hindustantimes.com/chandigarh/hooda-is-undisputed-king-of-haryana-s-sports/story-UdJVptWASi34coOnEm2jAO.html. Accessed on 29 November 2021.

sports academics in various disciplines.[21]

The momentum was continued by the Manohar Lal Khattar led BJP government. During the unveiling of the 'Haryana Physical Activities and Sports Policy-2015' the chief minister said, 'Besides conferring the right to employment on medal winners in recognized international competitions, the new policy would provide for an insurance scheme and concrete lifetime assistance to sportspersons in the shape of a pension scheme.'[22] An Olympic gold medallist now receives ₹6 crore and Asian gold medallist receives ₹3 crore. For a Commonwealth gold medal the government rewards winners with ₹1.5 crore. A very significant sum![23]

Apart from this, the government also offers jobs to sportspersons. Of course, it has other repercussions which need another discussion. But Haryana was able to tap into its pool of youngsters who propelled it to glory. As a consequence, Haryana became a top sporting state! For example, in the last Commonwealth Games one-third of the medal winners were from Haryana.

The results speak for themselves. Haryana has given Ravi Kumar Dahiya, Bajrang Punia, Vijender Singh, Saina

---

[21]Ibid.
[22]'Haryana CM Khattar unveils new sports policy; big bonuses for medal winners', *Hindustan Times*, 12 January 2015, https://www.hindustantimes.com/chandigarh/haryana-cm-khattar-unveils-new-sports-policy-big-bonuses-for-medal-winners/story-45IgErypTTDJCcAAJ8eGqI.html. Accessed on 29 November 2021.
[23]Ibid.

Nehwal, Yogeshwar Dutt, Sakshi Malik, Gagan Narang, Seema Punia, Vikas Yadav, Manjit Singh, Akhil Kumar, Phogat sisters, Sarita Mor, among others. The women's hockey team has a bulk of players from Haryana. The list goes on. And now there is the crowning glory—Neeraj Chopra.

3

Starting Young

'Chopra Brothers'

—Name of the Chopra family
WhatsApp group

Khandra

Vivek Singh is a simple, hard-working and humble bureaucrat in Haryana. His ever-smiling face has impacted many lives in the region, including Panipat, where I met him. As the zila parishad CEO, he was in charge of transforming the lives of people in rural Panipat. One day, I was in his office discussing ways to innovatively utilize the potential of self-help groups and non-profit organizations to revitalize the rural sector, when we decided that I would make a quick trip to Khandra, now more popular as Neeraj Chopra's village.

Khandra is a small village in the Madlauda block of Panipat district. From the Panipat mini-secretariat to Khandra is a distance of roughly 16 km, but the journey was not boring. Either by bus or by car, one makes way through the Panipat Bus stand, quickly followed by the main market of Panipat. All varieties of textiles, amongst other things are sold there. One takes a U-turn to start on Assandh Road. This road has been a vital artery for the town and people coming from the villages towards Jind, the neighbouring district. Always abuzz with traffic, one crosses important places, shops and junctions to other important places in town such as the Shivaji stadium. As one moves further, the city slowly fades away. I crossed canals and made my way through villages on the periphery of Panipat.

On the right, one crossed the St Mary's Convent School, the only convent school in the town and further down on the left is the Lepers' Colony. While the school has made history as one of the earliest schools to insist on speaking English within campus, the colony stands out for the stories of pain and grit inside it. Further down the road is Panipat Thermal Power Station. Come to think of it, Panipat is surrounded by some highly polluting industries. Towards the north is the Indian Oil Corporation Limited (IOCL) refinery; to the south is the National Fertilisers Limited; to the west is the coal-based thermal power station with other industries around it, and the textile cluster is scattered all over. Not a particularly great place to train or test one's lungs. The thermal power station colony is also home to the DAV School, one of the region's best sporting schools—it had horse riding, swimming, tennis and other sports facilities.

Further down via Madlauda and neighbouring village Thirana, one reaches Khandra. A quiet and peaceful village, Khandra is home to mostly farming families. It now resembles a village that is abuzz with action and activity. Just imagine that till a few years ago, it was a burrow where nothing singularly interesting happened. Residents would be involved in farming and keeping their cattle well-fed.

Now, however, everyone can direct you towards the Chopras—their new home and, quite significantly, the *baithak*! It is here, very close to the entry into the village that the family has developed a sit-out area with some rooms and a kitchen to welcome dignitaries and visitors. Early in the conversation with anyone in the family, one can understand that this family has worked hard to get out of the clutches of limited means and prospects. They are continuously reminding and training themselves to be grounded and level-headed—a tough job with all the money and fame that has flowed in though.

༄

Like other villages in the vicinity, Khandra is full of people from various castes such as Sunars, Chamars, Brahmins etc., but Rors mostly dominate the village. Out of the 12 to 14 Ror gotras, one that stands out now is the Chopra. The Chopra family of Khandra has become the fulcrum of major activity in the region. However, being invited and sought for a variety of things, the family is not trained in the process. It is slowly grasping and grappling with the media attention and public glare. Because all of this is new, everything is quite like a dream, a dream for which the entire family fought hard. And mind you, they don't forget to thank God for what they have been bestowed with. Neeraj's uncle—Bhim Chopra, for example, breaks into a quick prayer when he is reminded of where the family comes from, '*Main Bhagwaan se prarthana karta hoon; ki aisi khushiyaan har kisi ko de* (I pray to God; may He give such joy to everybody).'

Neeraj Chopra was born to Satish Kumar and Saroj Devi on 24 December 1997, in a joint family. Satish's brothers, Surender, Bhim and Sultan, have been living in the same household working and building things. Satish also has a sister who is married into a neighbouring village, Alupur.

As I write this, I have Surendar's WhatsApp conversation opened in front of me, and his display picture is a quote with two lions in the backdrop; it says, '*Registaan bhi hare ho jaate hain jab apne apnon ke saath khade ho jaate hain* (Even deserts turn green when near and dear ones stand together).' And as it turns out the family has done just that.

Chopra household has been living in this village for generations and always had limited means. The family lived with the very modest possessions of 5-acre land in Khandra and around 2.5-acre land in Thirana. After Satish's father injured himself at an early age, Satish left his studies and started working and taking care of the fields. Since he was the family's eldest son, the onus on him was still more enormous. Satish took care of the fields, and his wife carried the weight along. Satish consequently is a very modest man and is aware of the world outside of his own. Early on, his responsibilities were clear. He had to ensure that there was food on the table, and the family fought on! All those years of struggle show clearly on his wrinkled face and greying moustache. Satish's younger brother is Bhim, who is a heavyweight both on the weighing scale and as an impact on the starboy's life. He is the one you would see often interacting with the media and taking care of things in the family. He is also more entrepreneurial. While Satish took care of the fields, Bhim started looking for private jobs and contracts to contribute to the family. Over the years, Bhim continuously interacted with people in administration and business, and this experience also helped shape Neeraj's career. Bhim is also currently engaged in the business of supplying manpower and applying for private tenders and contracts.

Then there is Surender. Around a decade younger than Satish, Surender is the quieter one and wears the strategy hat in the house. While his brothers ensured that the family stayed afloat, Surender began understanding the modern ways of the world. He was always a passionate young man and wanted to excel in whatever he did. While at school, he participated in extra-curricular activities; striving hard to excel with the best performances. However, the daily challenges forced him to drop his passions and pursue something more practical that spelt money for sustenance. Finally, there was Sultan. The youngest of all the brothers, Sultan, is engaged in managing the fields with Satish.

All decisions of the family are taken collectively. The brothers sit together, talk about challenges and decide the way ahead. Hence, what Neeraj would do was not just deliberated upon by his father, Satish, but all his uncles too. I recollect sitting with them in a room together. When Satish was the only one present in the room, he noted that the other brothers, particularly Bhim and Surender, played a role in Neeraj's success. When Bhim joined, he laughed it off, saying it was Satish's hard work and Surender's push. And when Surender came in, he gestured towards his two elder brothers.

And that is the thing. The family had limited means, and they had to get out of the clutches of those challenges. So, everybody discussed together how they could accomplish their goals. They did not want the challenges they faced or had been facing to impede the growth of their children. The dictum of the family was 'we have to progress,' and they wanted to ensure that by whatever means possible.

I have to admit that this by itself became a great story. Joint family institutions have been witnessing a swift decline in response to modernization and urbanization.

Families are separating and moving out to different cities across India for a variety of reasons. This trend had been on for some time. However, there are still some families in Haryana which continue to live in this system and prosper. Here is a prime example.

Childhood

Neeraj was the first child in the family set-up. And as one would guess, the receiver of all the love and affection. As a child, he was '*gadra*' (raw) and understandably naughty. Many stories are attached to his playful antics in the village, which the family members shared with utmost joy. For instance, he once tied a knot to a buffalo's tail.

He enjoyed playing in the fields, making merry at home and being in the company of elders. A family member said, '*Ghar ka pehla tha. Hamaari jaan tha* (He was the first-born. And close to our hearts).' More so, Neeraj was particularly fond of his grandmother.

Natho Devi, Neeraj's grandmother and Satish's mother, was a woman of grit. She was a self-respecting woman and came from a family with comparatively more means. However, the family remembers that she never shied away from her responsibilities. Natho Devi stood shoulder to shoulder with her husband at every juncture. These principles that she taught everyone at home through her action made the family what it is today. She would suggest, '*Khud se karenge. Apne aap kuch nahiin hota* (Do it together. We can't accomplish anything by ourselves).' This dictum, in time, became the mantra of the family!

Grandma would also feed the young boy doodh, dahi, malai, makhan and ghee ensuring that the boy became a healthy and hearty kid. With this diet, of course, he would put on weight. Natho Devi, however, died in 2006. Neeraj then was around nine years old.

Neeraj was also borderline notorious and mischievous. Upset and irritated with the class teacher, he once threw his school bag into the village well. Returning home, he even shared the story at home. Some beating must have followed. Similarly, he once tried to shoo away bees at home. In the process, he accidentally set fire to a part of the house! His Uncle Bhim remembered, '*Shaam ko uski achi kuttaai hui.* (In the evening, he received a sound thrashing).'[24]

Another story that the family recollects fondly is how he would play with cows at home. He would take particular joy in tying knots to their tails. Uncle Sultan remembers, 'Once we heard him calling for help from the cattle shed. When we got there, we found him on the floor. He said he was trying to sit on the cow's back, but it pushed him down!'

Neeraj joined B.V.N. School in Madlauda where he studied till ninth standard. But by his own admission,

---

[24] Amsan, Andrew. 'Asian Games: Neeraj Chopra, Spearman from Khandra', *The Indian Express*, 29 July 2018, https://indianexpress.com/article/sports/asian-games/asian-games-neeraj-chopra-spearman-from-khandra-5281087/. Accessed on 29 November 2021.

Neeraj was not particularly fond of studies. It did not mean that he was not smart. He was a sharp young boy but reading books would not come naturally to him then, and he would rejoice in playing with other children in the village.

Choorma

The British Gazetteers record *choorma* as a food given as offerings to deities. That may be an opinion, but this is indeed true that rural Haryana's simple food habits have choorma as an essential food choice. Choorma is usually made by breaking fresh rotis into smaller pieces in a *paraant*. The bits are then mixed with ghee and gur (jaggery) for taste and turned into balls. Many variations now exist where one may use sugar or *khaand* in place of gur. Laced with ghee, choorma is a treat for so many of us. It is delicious and nutritious! Dieticians and nutritionists may have different opinions, but for the farming community, it was a regular affair. Moreover, the hard toil in a farmer's life ensures that the ghee was well digested.

During the 2019 Assembly polls, I remember travelling to a cluster of homes in the outskirts of Dighal village. Making way through open gutters, traditional sheds for cow feed, etc., I reached a house with two shiny black Maserati's parked in the shed. Our host was a young politician trying to make a dent in the opposition votes. Our host's mother made us choorma laced in ghee and gur along with a bowl of dal and some lassi. The meal was hearty and filling.

Neeraj, too has been particularly fond of choorma. After Neeraj won the gold at the Olympics, a swarm of journalists reached his home for stories and anecdotes. In one such interview, the ever-excited and short-of-words reporter asked what Neeraj's aunt would cook for him. She responded, 'He likes choorma. And when he comes back from Tokyo, he will get the same.' And the news was flashed all over!

More so, even the prime minister who hosted a banquet for the Olympians served Neeraj some choorma. A coy champion, Neeraj ate it with a spoon, maintaining the decorum of the function. But ask choorma lovers—the real joy of eating it is by hand.

Madlauda

*'Khaake Makhan—Malaaiyaan hua wadaa baliye,
Taaiyon raub rakha filmy star warga.'*[25]

(He has grown up relishing butter and cream,
Hence has an attitude like that of a film star)

As Neeraj continued receiving the lion's share of *makhan-malai*, he started gaining weight. By the time he was

---

[25]Illegal Weapon by Garry Sandhu and Jasmine Sandlas, *YouTube*, https://www.youtube.com/watch?v=H7_yY3yr-jE. Accessed on 29 November 2021.

around 12 years old, he was grossly overweight at 75 kgs. Some journalists have even marked it to be around 90 kg. Further, the family recollected that when he wore a bright new kurta, his peers began calling him Sarpanch ji! Sarpanch is the head of the village and a respected person in the community. But in the case of Neeraj, it became more of a joke because of his rotund disposition. And it bothered the family.

At this juncture, another discussion began in the family. Surender, who was then around 30 years old, was looking for options to help the family step out of its mould. The world around them had been progressing; people were rising socially and financially. He was indeed thinking of what could be done so that the family makes marked progress.

This discussion started to happen in the family meetings too, as now the family had started to make ends meet. This may be a good start but something else must be thought of to make the leap onto the high table. Everyone in the family agreed.

But what could be it? In 2008, the Summer Olympics were held in Beijing, China. Shooter Abhinav Bindra won the first-ever individual gold medal for India. Hailing from Chandigarh, the shared capital of Haryana and Punjab, he became a star. The other two Haryanvis to bring home a medal were boxer Vijender Singh and wrestler Sushil Kumar. The fame and laurels that they received back home were unparalleled. Similarly, Haryanvi sportsmen were excelling in different fields, winning cash awards as well as job guarantees as rewards. This could be it then, thought the family.

But Neeraj was unfit for any sport at that juncture. He was enrolled in a gymnasium at Madlauda for a few months. This is where he began his workouts. He began training his heart out, but a lot of that time was spent emptying machines or carrying weights for the seniors in the gym. A few months later, the gymnasium closed. His uncles began exploring other options.

Surender, at this time, had gotten himself engaged in the network marketing business. He had become a partner at Forever Living Products. He would travel around, get into conversations with people, learn valuable motivational lessons and look for options for young Neeraj. At one such event he met Jitender Jaglan.

Jitender was then a highly motivated javelin thrower who had begun training young students for physical fitness. He would train young boys and girls, give them physical fitness lessons and help them stay in shape. Around this time, he had also joined a gymnasium as a trainer in Model Town, Panipat.

Jitender, who is also fondly called Jitu, was a keen student of nutrition. At one event, he recalls asking the main speaker some typical questions from a sportsman and trainer's point of view, which the former could not answer. Surender was also at the event. As the session closed, an impressed Surender got into conversation with Jitu to understand more about nutrition and Jitu's expertise.

The discussion was relatively simple. Discussing the height, weight and body proportions of Neeraj, Surender wanted to be sure if Jitu knew the basics and Neeraj could gain height. In effect, he was assessing if he would make a good coach for Neeraj. As it happened, Neeraj soon joined coach Jitu, who was given a simple task—to not worry about the money. 'Please tell us what you need. But ensure that our boy becomes healthy and fit,' he said.

Since the Madlauda gymnasium days were over, Neeraj had gained his weight and needed a real fix. And with that, Neeraj came to Panipat.

Shivaji Stadium

In the centre of modern Panipat is a large ground named after Chhatrapati Shivaji Maharaj, whose descendant Marathas had fought bravely in the Third Battle of Panipat in 1761. The stadium has for the longest time been a centre of all sporting and other recreational activities. A rather disappointing thing pointed out by many successful sportsmen who trained there is that the ground is not just a sports stadium. It has been used as Dussehra ground and for setting stalls for selling firecrackers during Diwali. From the Republic Day parade to other prominent district events, many ceremonies had taken place here. Organizers of these events would invariably dig up the track and the parts of the field to install poles, making the players susceptible to injuries.

Sprinter Ravinder Antil, a national level athlete in the early 1990s, never fails to hide his disappointment in this regard. So does Munish, another sportsman who practised there. The sports facilities are quite inadequate and whatever is available is in such a shabby state that it poses more risks than advantages. The sportspersons quite clearly make their way through this turmoil. Others, however, would get injured and be forced to step out.

As a youngster, I had played cricket and later practised basketball there. My grandfather Chaudhary Vijay Kumar was the first deputy commissioner of Panipat district and had a vital role in giving the stadium the much-required push decades ago. A stone plaque in the corner of the grounds remembers the same. But much more needed to be done to make it a successful breeding ground for sportspersons.

The stadium is a multi-sporting facility for basketball, cricket, football, softball, hockey, running track, volleyball etc., all congregating in one place. In the evenings, it is a sight to see scores of Hero Honda Splendour motorcycles lined up outside the gate and bicycles locked outside the premises or leaning against the walls of the stadium—as their owners toiled with tears and sweat inside.

The stadium is also a vital pit stop in what is now popular as the Ring Road of Model Town, Panipat. It has been a *geri* route for quite some time now. Young boys and girls on scooters, motorcycles and cars can be seen leisurely driving around! There have been instances where I heard the pompous ones in fancy cars passing remarks about the sportspersons. For weren't we all told—'*Kheloge-koodoge toh hoge kharaab!* (Fun and games will only ruin you).'

Regardless, this stadium now welcomes everyone with a nice flex poster of the boy who trained here in early 2011—Olympian gold medallist Neeraj Chopra. This is where Uncle Surender left Neeraj in the hands of Coach Jitu.

Because Surender approached him so honestly and straightforwardly, Jitu ensured that young Neeraj received many individual classes and his exercise routines gradually picked up.

Jitu realized that a quick transition into high-intensity workouts could injure the young boy. At first, Neeraj's training only focused on cardio exercises for reducing weight. The training was patient and effective. Neeraj would do long-distance runs and short sprints. On the pavilion stairs, he would do jumps and skips on one leg and two. Push-ups and pull-ups were followed by some ab crunches. At the peak of his drill, he would be doing 10 to 12 rounds of the 400-m track. Jitu would take him to the gymnasium on the left, right outside the stadium where the coach was employed for some weight exercises.

Jitu remembers that Neeraj was always a hard worker. He never said no to exercise. He was a young boy raring to go. The results, hence, were remarkable, and in six months Neeraj lost around 10–15 kg.

Hence, in late 2010 and early 2011, Neeraj was exposed to the Shivaji Stadium. By his own admission, Neeraj was not aware of a javelin until he reached the stadium. When his uncles or family talked about playing some game, a rather natural response would be wrestling or kabaddi. Neeraj, of course, had the body for both sports. He was heavy, flexible and agile. Wrestling and kabaddi are also *'zameeen se jude huey'* sports (games linked to rural India). Many young boys from villages chose to play the sport. However, this star in the making was not destined for either.

༄

Sports education at the school and district levels is abysmal. The system suffers from an acute absence of infrastructure and opportunities ensuring that no fresh spark is ignited. That is probably, the reason why most successful sportspersons from the region come from humble backgrounds—life is already tough, and there is no other avenue to get out of the rut.

At the school level, there are no coaches but only physical education teachers who are more responsible for maintaining discipline in schools rather than instilling 'sporting discipline'. Earlier, the objective of schools was to produce citizens who could join the workforce. In this regard, sports in Haryana and India offered hardly anything.

A change, of course, set in when the big corporates and advertising gurus joined the space. Sporting successes became an industry and the player, a star. A perfect emulation of the American way of doing things!

This was a blessing for the sportsperson. For now, the sportsperson could focus on the game and their funding and finance could be taken care of. The ones who could not get any sponsorships could do well with the prize money. Hence, financial consideration was a critical motivation.

What this has achieved is that schools all over have also started to scout for talent. They now provide scholarships to the bright ones and provide a platform to sports stars in the making.

Moreover, a considerable focused effort was also made by the government in the last few years to improve the sporting infrastructure. More opportunities and incentives have been able to revitalize the space.

4

En Route to Panipat

Panipat is an industrial town about 100 km from modern Delhi's Khan Market. It was an important centre during the medieval ages with a distinctive Islamic and Sufi culture. It was also here that three very significant battles took place that defined the medieval history of India.

We can argue that maybe that is the reason why Haryana has suffered for ages. It is on these lands that the battles for the Delhi throne took place. While Delhi became the land of glory, Haryana was slashed and chopped, thanks to the anarchy.

The three battles of 1526, 1556 and 1761 have divided epochs between them. Yet, the modern town of Panipat lost out to Karnal. Karnal had become an important centre during the East India Company days, which had established a cantonment there before shifting to Ambala. Even during the 1857 struggle for Independence, it involved Panipat's Bu Ali Shah Qalandar shrine.

Haryana state was formed on 1 November 1966, and Panipat town was then part of the Karnal district in the state. The city was first separated from Karnal and made a district in 1989. It was, however, re-merged with Karnal in July 1991 and ultimately re-established as a district on 1 January 1992. The district has five tehsils today: Panipat, Samalkha, Israna, Bapoli and Madlauda.

Khandra village has now become the centre of gravity of Madlauda tehsil. Around 16 km on the Assandh Road, Khandra is inhabited by approximately 2,500 people today. A nondescript village with no access to a gymnasium and inhabited chiefly by farming families, it was a sight to behold the day Neeraj won the gold.

Choosing the Game or Vice Versa

By the second quarter of 2011, Neeraj was in shape, and the conversation about a game of choice gained ground again. Top sports that have always caught Haryanvi attention, such as wresting and kabaddi, were discussed. But Surender thought that these sports were physically draining, and the player was prone to many injuries. He may have been wrong because javelin is also a technical sport in which the thrower may get injured, but the knowledge of this sport was somewhat limited. Further, Surender believed that these sports also lead to weak knees or ankles later in life. Hence, the discussion was hot.

For more than a month, Jitu put Neeraj through various drills. Neeraj would play volleyball, long jumps, throwing drills, etc. But the question remained unanswered.

Enter Krishan Mittan

Krishan Mittan is now middle-aged and working in a department of the Indian Railways. He looked like a sophisticated professional, but his face suggested that he had been through enough turmoil. Moreover, he was now seldom seen in the Shivaji Stadium, but took part in numerous sports conversations; he was a well-known face.

Krishan came from a family with very limited means. Since his youth, he knew that sports, discipline and hard work were the only way to make this life worthwhile. In the early 1990s, after moving from one sport to another, he settled on the javelin throw. When Krishan trained at the Shivaji Stadium, the two prominent coaches there were Rampal Sangwan and O.P. Simhar. Sangwan used to be a thrower himself in his heydays. Under their guidance and tutelage, Krishan developed his skill set and became a good javelin thrower.

Javelin, unlike today, was not a popular sport then. A few players had limited to no access to facilities such as coaches, nutrition and implements. Under these circumstances,

Krishan steadily brought together a community of javelin throwers. He was a medallist in numerous sporting events and, in time, assured himself a government job through his sporting successes. People who knew him recollected fondly that Krishan had risen from abject surroundings and now sat well in a government job, inspiring many others in the process. And then a way to help Neeraj showed up.

Neeraj's Uncle Bhim Chopra was then associated in a professional capacity with Millennium School in Panipat. Krishan's wife, too, worked there. Bhim had noticed Krishan's connections to Panipat's sporting arena and approached him.

Krishan reminisced that Bhim was then proactively seeking suggestions for young Neeraj. With some well-guided inputs, javelin throw became a feasible option.

Neeraj was asked to head to Shivaji Stadium where a next-gen talent was already training. Here, Neeraj met his seniors, who became his friends on his journey to javelin stardom.

Another story that Jitu recollected was how he found that Neeraj had a knack for the sport. Himself a javelin thrower, Jitu was a part of a small group of javelin throwers from Panipat and neighbouring villages.

Jitu noted that Neeraj always practised hard. He would be running long distances and in no time became part of the stadium's javelin circuit. Jitu was a javelin thrower himself and was introduced to the game by Mittan. Before that, Jitu used to throw the shot-put. But having injured his tail bone once, he made a gradual shift towards the javelin.

Since Jitu was part of the circuit, his young star was also introduced to the game and the group. Neeraj would be running and circuit-training while others were teaching each other the game.

One day, Sunny and another javelin thrower, Arun handed Neeraj the javelin. Neeraj was asked to show his best effort. To their surprise, Neeraj packed it well in his hand and released it nicely. A good sign!

The throw convinced Jitu and Surender. And a consensus evolved. Neeraj was about to begin his pursuit of javelin glory.

Friends for Life

Shivaji stadium then had a small number of people who used to practise the javelin throw. All of them were in some way or the other trained by Krishan. He would go to the stadium, notice what the young boys were doing, who was throwing seriously and who was just fooling around. He would later reprimand or compliment the young men.

Sunny

One of those young men training there was Jagdeep or who is more popularly called Sunny. Having gained weight now, Sunny was very athletic in his prime. His throws were something to watch in that stadium. Krishan used to stay in the same neighbourhood as Sunny when the latter was still in his early teens. Krishan would push him to try his hand at sports, and Sunny with his grounded principles practised the sport with all his heart. After winning numerous medals for the state, he was selected for the SAI training centre in Hisar, which was very popular for javelin in those days. It was also particularly close to another sporting hub—Bhiwani.

After finishing three years at SAI Centre, Hisar, Sunny, returned to train in Panipat, his hometown, with other friends such as Monu.

Monu

Another person in the stadium then was Jaiveer Chowdhary, better known as Monu. With chiselled features and steely eyes, Monu was a dashing javelin thrower. Hailing from Binjhal village, he had started to play with the javelin at an early age. Monu and Sunny were colleagues and competitors. After a lot of hard work he built his craft and learnt numerous things in the process. However, laurels always evaded Monu. Despairingly, nearly all his friends said that Monu was the unlucky one. He worked tremendously hard and was strategic at every step. He was conscious about his diet and the nuances of the sport. However, whenever he performed at an event, something went awry. One could almost feel the pain when his friends shared his story. He would throw well in training, but the minute he entered a competition, he would come up short.

Sunny and Monu were doing their off-season training

when junior Neeraj entered the arena. Holding water bottles, picking javelins at the landing circuit and helping with other chores, Neeraj received their suggestions and guidance on training. It turned them into a closely-knit group.

~

When the discussion over Neeraj's game began, Surender also had a chat with Monu. It was this conversation, Surender recollected, which filled him with hope. If it was going to be a throwing sport for Neeraj, it could be the javelin. Another thing that worked was the fact that javelin was a less heard of sport. Surender believed that since not many people knew about the sport, the competition would not be as fierce. Interestingly, that is how Neeraj's progress seemed!

Parvinder Singh Choudhary 'Saab'

Another member of the group was Parvinder, who is fondly called Saab. Saab is a short and stocky man who had at one point been one of the top performers of this stadium group. Saab was also a native of Binjhal village and neighbour of Monu's. Saab never failed to mention that Monu taught him the basics and trained everyone in the process. But his mentees quickly surpassed his best efforts which contrary to what could be expected, did not pinch Monu.

Learning the Basics

Neeraj, the youngest addition to the javelin club, began imbibing the basics of the sport from his seniors. These are the same seniors he never fails to credit and acknowledge for his achievements.

The Shivaji Stadium has two big gate entrances. One opens towards the Ring Road and the other towards the road to Dr M.K.K. School. The javelin run-up track was adjoining the basketball court, separated only by a section of running track, on the school side of the stadium. Seniors would throw their javelins with all their might, and Neeraj would carefully observe them, learning the art in the process. Since he was also the youngest, he would be the one on the landing side of the stadium to pull out the sticks from the ground. He would learn the descent patterns and how a good javelin sticks out from the ground.

In no time, his javelin training commenced. But remember, none of this came easy.

Nothing Came Easy, But Familial Love Worked

As one browses through Neeraj's journey to fame it is easy to gloss over his turmoil. In early 2011, Neeraj was a little over 13 years old. He was travelling around 15 km from his village daily to reach the stadium. He would often accompany his uncles Surender and Bhim or take a bus.

The family focused on making ends meet and improving

their financial status to ensure it did not disrupt Neeraj's training. So, while they would be confident that they would drop him off in time for his training, they were not sure they would pick him up!

These stories of struggle are also joyfully remembered by all. For instance, one day, everyone had reached home to find out that the boy had not returned. They launched a search and discovered that he had been left behind at the bus stand! When family members went to pick him up, they found him fast asleep. After much good-natured teasing, the family realized that he inherited the habit of sleeping anywhere from his father, Satish! They both could sleep anywhere and at any time.

Satish was not coy about another thing. His most important job was to ensure that the lack of money did not disrupt the boy's training. The family had to ensure that he received a proper diet—milk, curds, ghee and different fruits. Uncles would take him to train and observe his progress. They would speak to his friends, seek suggestions on steps ahead and be sure that their boy was heading in the right direction.

Thanks to all these efforts, Neeraj was raring to explore the Olympic sport of javelin further.

Learning Javelin

In javelin throw, an athlete flings a javelin, about 2.5 m (8'2") in length, with all his or her might to the longest distance. The athlete runs through a pre-determined area to gain momentum, and the one who throws the javelin to the maximum distance wins the event.

The International Association of Athletics Federations (IAAF) defines the proportions of the javelin (size, shape, minimum weight and centre of gravity). Typically, in international competitions, men throw a javelin which weighs 800 g. The javelin has a tip (the front end), a grip (where the athlete holds the javelin) and a tail (rear end). The grip is about 5.9 inches wide and made of a cord.

Unlike other throwing events, the IAAF rules also govern the techniques and unorthodox ways are disallowed. The javelin must be held by the grip and carried and thrown overhand, above the athlete's shoulder or upper arm. The athlete cannot turn completely around so that his back faces the direction of the throw. Hence, one cannot spin and hurl the implement such as a discuss thrower. The spin and hurl was experimented and attempted long back but it was banned through rule specifications because of the sheer risk and danger.

The thrower has a runway about four-metre wide and at least 30 m in length, ending in a curved arc from where the distance of the throw is measured. This distance is used for a run-up to gain momentum before the throw. Because the athlete must come to a halt before the arc-line, it limits the maximum speed the thrower can achieve.

The javelin is then hurled with maximum speed from the throwing arm towards the 'sector'. The sector covers an area of 28.96 degrees extending outwards from the arc-line. A legal throw is thrown before the arc line and falls within the sector. The distance of the throw is measured from the throwing arc to the point where the tip of javelin lands, measured down to the nearest centimetre.

In most competitions, there are six rounds. In every round, each athlete gets to make one throw. At the end of all the rounds, officials compare each athlete's best or longest throw. The one with the longest throw in all rounds is considered the winner. In the case of a tie, officials compare the second-best throws.

Fundamentals

Javelin is a game of overhead throws. Like with a cricket ball, it is thrown with a single arm. One is using the cricket ball analogy for quick understanding of the subject. Otherwise, a cricket ball weighs an average 160 g in contrast to the 800 g of the javelin.

In both sports, the athlete is allowed a run-up and much like a cricket bowler cannot cross the 'bowling crease', the javelin thrower cannot cross the throwing arc-line. Javelin is also an overhead throwing event, and throwing a ball in the same manner is usually the first step towards a javelin throw. Interestingly, many exercises for top throwers utilize the ball fundamentals.

There are usually three different ways to grip the javelin:

i) Index finger grip
ii) Fork grip
iii) Finnish grip

The release of a javelin has two crucial aspects: velocity and angle. The release velocity increases over time with training. The athlete attains his or her top speed in around 10 steps and then throws the javelin. This velocity is attained with an optimal magnitude of a release angle.

The release angle of a javelin is usually between 32 and 40 degrees, depending upon the implement. Another term used is the yaw angle, or the angle seen from behind the throw. It should be as small as possible.

Throws

To prepare himself for a javelin throw, a young athlete usually begins with a standing throw. In the case of a right arm thrower, the shoulder is stretched a few times. The left foot is in front of the left hip, the right arm is raised high over the head and slightly bent and relaxed. The right elbow stays at ear level. The javelin is raised, and there is eye contact with the tip. Before the throw, the hand makes a final effort, much like a 'whipping' action, to further increase the velocity.

Then there is the one-step throw drill. Here, the javelin is pulled back with the shoulder as far as possible from the torso. The javelin is still parallel to the ground and faces the direction of the throw. This position is popularly known as the T position. The right-hand thrower then steps forward with the left foot and throws the javelin aggressively.[26] It is critical to keep the left arm close and in front. Also, the left leg should block and be adequately grounded to form a strong base for the throw.

Another thing needed for a strong throw is the ability to transfer all power onto the throwing hand. It is done by attaining a C-position wherein the hand and shoulder are high enough so that the body, left leg and throwing hand (right hand) will make a 'C' shape.[27]

∾

Then there is the running throw, exercised by professionals and competitors. It usually starts with a four-stride approach, but when the athlete understands it better, 10 stride approach is practised. This approach is used by most senior athletes in their routine practice schedule. The length of the run-up generally varies between 17–21 m. It is essential to understand this process because through rigorous practice in Panipat followed by Panchkula, Neeraj achieved almost perfection and his throws began crossing a distance of 70 m.

---

[26]'Javelin Throw—How to Play?', *Tutorials Point*, https://www.tutorialspoint.com/javelin_throw/javelin_throw_how_to_play.htm. Accessed on 29 November 2021.
[27]Ibid.

- Keep both your feet together and hold the javelin above shoulder level.
- The feet must face towards the sector. Stretch the throwing arm and ready the left leg for a sudden block that comes at the end of the run-up. With the right foot first start making forward strides.
- Lift the knees high during the run and try gaining maximum sprint velocity in the first five strides. During the fifth and sixth strides, pull the javelin back along with the shoulders.
- By the seventh stride, the javelin should be back with maximum strain. During this period, the hips completely turn clockwise, and the right leg crosses over the left leg. Hence this stride is often termed as the 'crossover'. This is a very crucial move. Training for it could hurt the ankle or damage anything else seriously.
- The impulse stride (the last before stride) should be as long as possible, and at last, with a powerful stride, complete the throwing action.

One must note a couple of other things. For the right arm thrower, the left leg has to be very strong. It not only helps accelerate to the maximum speed but has to bring the athlete to a sudden halt. When the left leg has to enact the blocking action, it must be firmly on the ground until the javelin is thrown. Further, the left leg should be as straight as possible to give an effective block.

Another important thing is that the athlete should attain a T position. Right before the throw, the athlete should keep the level of both shoulders the same. They must quickly recover after the implement is thrown by landing on the right foot before the arc.

The thrower must balance between speed and action because with higher speed, one can take an incorrect step, and the javelin may land outside the sector. Further, during the crossover, the feet may entangle, or the javelin may touch the ground and disrupt the movement which should otherwise be seamless.[28]

Javelin throwing is a complicated discipline. A thrower, and more specifically a javelin thrower, must draw all power from different parts of the body. It is commonly said, 'In javelin, 40 per cent is your upper body and 60 per cent is the lower body)' This loosely means that 40 per cent of the upper body and 60 per cent of the lower body plays a role for a good javelin throw. This is where s/he draws power from.

Javelin coach Garry Calvert says, 'There is no other event where you have to sprint as fast as you can then come to a stop in one step while simultaneously flinging an object. There are just so many ways to hurt yourself.'[29]

---

[28]Ibid.

[29]Selvaraj, Jonathan. 'India's Latest Athletics Sensation Neeraj Chopra Is Brimming with Natural Talent', *The Indian Express*, 28 February 2016, https://indianexpress.com/article/sports/sport-others/neeraj-chopra-javelin-south-asian-games-garry-calvert/. Accessed on 29 November 2021.

Training at Panipat

Now Neeraj became a part of a happy and ambitious group, playing and learning all by themselves. All of them were highly motivated. Either they would win laurels or they would get a government job.

It must have been a sight; young boys training each other and themselves without the support of any coach. The only people to prepare them were the seniors in the group. By the second quarter of 2011, Neeraj had started dabbling with the javelin.

Sunny had gotten back from the SAI Centre, Hisar, and along with Monu, they were training very hard. It was their off-season. Hence, the only focus was on building their strength and giving their very best in the upcoming events. Neeraj was fortunate to see these seniors perform to the peak of their ability.

However, logistical challenges continued to hamper his growth. Seeing the challenges in travelling to and from the village, Neeraj shifted to Panipat for a while. Paralympian Narender took a room in Kachcha camp, Panipat, to train better. Kachcha camp, on the Assandh Road, Panipat is a colony with small quarters. The name suggests that it was a refugee camp for people coming from Pakistan after the Partition.

This shift was able to facilitate training for the young boy. His parents did not want him to leave because of his age but the desire to better himself trumped all apprehensions. It became a hostel of sorts for the group too. Monu, Sunny, Narender and Neeraj took breaks here. Sunny would return home in Panipat, though. This stay was for about two months, around the middle of 2011. Notably, within a few months, Neeraj had improved enough to win a bronze in the district championships.[30]

Baba Coach

The city of Jalandhar in Punjab is also home to another javelin 'fighter' who became another small part of Neeraj's journey. Remembered as Baba Coach, Gurdeep Singh, was a javelin thrower in his teens and performed some good feats with his limited means. Thanks to his performances in the school nationals, where he won silver medals, he was inducted into the Punjab Police and continued playing the sport. However, fate had something else in store for him.

In 1998, Gurdeep visited Germany to improve his throws. He was making considerable progress crossing the 75-m mark. However, one evening after the invitation meet in Germany where he threw his personal best of around 76 m, his life went topsy-turvy.

---

[30]Selvaraj, Jonathan. 'Neeraj Chopra Creates History to Become First Indian World Champion in Athletics', *The Indian Express* 28 February 2016, https://indianexpress.com/article/sports/sport-others/neeraj-chopra-creates-history-becomes-first-indian-world-champion-in-athletics-2932114/. Accessed on 29 November 2021.

Gurdeep was cycling back home from the meet on the route he usually took. It was shorter and was not the highway. His racing cycle sprinted well until, at a turn, Gurdeep's bike hurtled 50 to 60 feet downhill from a cliff, and he crash-landed in a field. The handle of the cycle hit his spine, making him immobile. Throughout the night, Gurdeep screamed for help, but nobody heard his cries. Gurdeep remembered the day vividly because his life changed forever after that.

The next morning, he was spotted, air-lifted and taken to a hospital. Gurdeep kept begging, *'Mujhe bas mere pairon par khada kar do'* (Please just help me get back on my feet). However, he arrived in India in a wheelchair. He did the rounds of the doctors, but nothing worked. But it was Gurdeep's willpower, courage and spirit, and numerous physiotherapy sessions that slowly saw an improvement in his condition.

In 2000, his friend Bahadur Singh took him around on his Bullet and they went to the stadium. At the break of the century, Gurdeep kickstarted his sporting life all over again. Since then, he has gradually reorganized his life. He is now a coach and trains youngsters for fitness. Interestingly, coach Ratan Chand blessed him in the early 1990s declaring that he would be called 'Baba'.

Hence, Neeraj along with Monu visited Baba Coach for training sessions. They learnt a few things and spent around two weeks there before coming back to Panipat. Other boys in the group also visited Baba Coach sometime in 2012. Baba remembers the boys as hardworking fellows from Panipat.

Neeraj, however, returned to Panipat and began the village-to-Shivaji Stadium drill all over again. Monu suggested, '*Neeraj idhar se tera theek nahiin hai aanaa jaane. Tu ek kaam kar, Saab se baat kar and udhar (Panchkula) ja.*' (From here this coming and going isn't working for you. You do one thing, speak with Saab and move to Panchkula).

∽

On the side, as we close the Panipat bit, Neeraj was hooked to the javelin from day one, by his own admission. Those friends and seniors who had seen him making this trajectory from a newbie to a sensation told me clearly that he was a 'natural'. And, on top of it, he was most humble on the ground. He was ever ready to put in the hard work and took all suggestions positively. He always listened to his seniors and, in all honesty, deserves to be where he is today.

Saab, who currently works in the Railways, recollected that Neeraj had all the qualities to become a top athlete and bask in the glory. Saab knew it back then, and consequently pushed Neeraj harder.

Hence, in 2011, Neeraj Chopra picked the javelin as his sport and started training hard. He admitted recently that he had no idea he wanted to get into the sport or practice it, as it has such a limited lifeline. But here we are.

Sunny, who humbly took what life threw at him, now runs a store and factory for sporting goods in Panipat. The perennial 'mast-maula' Sunny smiled when he reminisced about Neeraj's good heart and his humbleness. Even after all the laurels, he treats all of his friends and co-athletes with love and respect. More power to this lot!

Monu, on the other hand, was hard to reach. His impact on Neeraj's life would be evident much later, but the truth is that for any consultation and support, Monu was always available for Neeraj. There was turmoil in his life too, but he remained Neeraj's confidant.

༄

By this time, mobile phones and YouTube had started entering the lives of young stars. I was sitting with Jitender in a restaurant close to the Shivaji Stadium, where he shared some anecdotes. He was a highly motivated man a decade ago and thought that Neeraj needed inspiration too. So, he gave Neeraj a Kingston pen drive with videos of top Javelin throwers to study. I asked him if they had a computer, and he said Surender was always ready to do anything that could positively impact Neeraj's training.

5

Becoming a Pro

Saab to Sports Nursery

anchkula is around 150 km from Panipat. The city is part of the grander Tricity that encompasses Chandigarh, Mohali and Panchkula. Since the founding of the state, Chandigarh has been the shared capital as a Union Territory. The two states also share the joint capital complex and the high court. While the two states argued their cases for Chandigarh's possession, Punjab built Mohali and Haryana made Panchkula in line with Chandigarh's plan.

Today Panchkula houses the most important offices in the state and is also usually the first grantee of state schemes. The city also houses the Tau Devi Lal Sports Complex named after India's former deputy prime minister. Devi Lal was a tall, rugged politician who fought for Haryana's rights. He became the chief minister of the state in 1977 and again a decade later. His tenure as the chief minister was, however, cut short both times.

In time, his family took up the political mantle amidst a lot of chaos and infighting. When Devi Lal died in 2001, his son Om Prakash Chautala was the chief minister of Haryana. Chautala ensured that he preserved his father's memory in the minds and hearts of Haryanvis. As a consequence, he erected statues and renamed stadiums in his father's name. In time, he immortalized Devi Lal.

The sports nursery was at the Devi Lal sports complex, a multi-sports complex where players gathered to work and build their skills to reach the next level. It was a ground full of motivation and opportunities. Young athletes from all districts of Haryana and some from Punjab also trained here. Thanks to his medal at the nationals, Saab was selected for the nursery at Panchkula.

Saab began his training here. The facility offered accommodation and food along with sound equipment and a training ground. In return, the athletes poured their sweat and tears into the sport. The conversations and the gang, however, were not left behind. Sunny, Neeraj, Monu and others were all apprised of the facilities at Panchkula. Hence, when it was suggested that Neeraj come to Panchkula. Saab agreed and reached out to the nursery coach.

Naseem Coach

Naseem Ahmed or Naseem coach is a proud man today. He was then the coach of the nursery when Neeraj, then around 14, came to Panchkula. Saab had reached out to Naseem and told him about the young boy who was showing great potential. Naseem decided to conduct some trials and decide.

Although Naseem had little to share with the throwers, the accommodation and good facilities for training was more than what the boys could ask for. In such circumstances, Neeraj joined the Panchkula sports nursery and stayed there for the next few years.

Neeraj recollects, 'Naseem coach allowed me to stay in the hostel. Panchkula, Chandigarh are costly cities to live in. In those days it was tough to live and train there. So Naseem coach said, "Don't worry much. Stay at the hostel. Continue your training. Work hard." This was of great help.'

Neeraj Chopra cleared the entrance a few months later, made Panchkula his home and trained there till 2015.

Athletes fondly remember Naseem as someone always ready to help them. He motivated them and went out of his way to ensure that a player under him achieved glory with some effort. Although a 400-m sprinter in his prime, he used to help provide facilities to all athletes in the nursery.

Naseem fondly recallls the day when a young Neeraj came to the sports academy. 'When he joined the academy, how much could you expect from a 13-year-old? He would throw around 55 m. But he had this natural ability to judge the angles correctly. In javelin throws, angles made all the difference. While most of the others would struggle even to hit 50 m, he would gradually increase his distance by two to three metres.'[31]

∽

Neeraj would train hard with his seniors. He would learn all the minute details, observe each step, take notes and measure his success. Neeraj's fundamentals were already strong, thanks to the Shivaji Stadium group. What set him apart was his desire to improve every day. Rather than wasting time loitering around, Neeraj, at that young an age, would pester seniors to watch javelin-throwing videos—even the best Olympic throws. He was gradually training his mind to focus and achieve the impossible.

The 'Shivaji group' in the hostel would live together and train together. Neeraj's passion for the game was remarkable. He would always have questions about technique, grips, etc. Since Panchkula was a better facility, exposure to imported, top-quality javelins also happened for the young boys. The

---

[31] Baparnash, Tridib. 'Training with Long-Distance Runners Helped Neeraj Chopra Gain Strength, Says Childhood Coach Naseem Ahmad', *The Times of India*, 9 August 2021, https://timesofindia.indiatimes.com/sports/tokyo-olympics/india-in-tokyo/training-with-long-distance-runners-helped-neeraj-chopra-gain-strength-says-childhood-coach-naseem-ahmad/articleshow/85169902.cms. Accessed on 29 November 2021.

bond only grew, and each day brought new memories for Narender and Saab. Neeraj also began cooking, living the best hostel life! His pulao would top any made by a Michelin star chef.[32]

In time, Neeraj's craft improved along with his strength and stamina. In no time, young Neeraj made remarkable progress. He understood complicated moves such as the angle required for a good throw. Sunny recollected that it seemed as if Neeraj knew from that age that all the energy must be transferred rightly onto the javelin at the release.

Coach YouTube

It is imperative to remember that Naseem Ahmad was not primarily a javelin coach. In his journey so far, Neeraj had only been trained by seniors who were coaches, brothers and friends—all clubbed into one. In Panchkula as well, dependency was more on YouTube videos of international javelin stars and his seniors. YouTube became his coach! He would watch videos of star thrower and record-holder Jan Železný and copy his technique.

Neeraj would also watch javelin throwing videos in slow motion, obsessively to focus his mind. Not just others, he

---

[32] Sharma, Nitin. 'Former Coach Recalls Chubby Neeraj Chopra With A Notebook, Now An Olympic Gold', *The Indian Express*, 8 August 2021, https://indianexpress.com/article/olympics/former-coach-recalls-the-chubby-kid-with-a-notebook-now-an-olympic-gold-medallist-neeraj-chopra-7443442/. Accessed on 29 November 2021.

would also observe himself and try understanding what worked and what did not. Even in the absence of javelin coaches, he would continue to improve and the credit goes to this habit. And because he was improving, he believed it worked.

∽

But that was not it. Look at it from this side: Indian sports infrastructure in 2011 was already in shambles. There was a paucity of funds, and store managers were usually reticent about lending goods bought during the Commonwealth Games 2010. This had begun to change slightly but was still grossly inadequate, considering India wanted to become a global powerhouse. It was not just the availability of stadia or implements but the critical shortage of coaches that was the bane of a sportsperson's lives in those times.

In the midst of that, could one understand the importance of a 'Naseem Coach'? For a player struggling to make it with whatever limited resources Neeraj had, Naseem helped young athletes with full freedom to practice. He motivated and inspired them to better themselves every day, shared exercising drills and gave them the confidence—*'Karo. Jamm ke mehnat karo* (Do it. Just work hard).'

And the results showed. Naseem recalled, 'Every time he (Neeraj) touched a newer distance, he would note it down. For him, what mattered the most was to set new targets every day. In his free time, he would be with a book in his hostel room; he was never an outdoor person.'[33]

Naseem also helped him with his drills. Javelin is not only about distance, it also needs stamina and strength for a proper run-up. 'If you have the wrong run-up, you might end up injuring your ankle at the release point. There was never a flaw with his throwing, but we had to work on his technique and strength. That was the reason why we made him train along with the long-distance runners. Since he had this tall frame, he could afford a wide last stride that gave him the momentum for a smooth throw. He had that advantage. We would also start with two-three run-ups and gradually increase it to a full run-up by the end of the day.'[34]

'Panchkula remembers him as a sharp boy. Coming from rural Haryana, he had the hunger to do well and become a top-notch athlete. Three-four young javelin throwers had come from Panipat with him to excel in the sport as there was no javelin equipment in Panipat's academies. He had previously won two or three tournaments at the district and state level,' said the coach, posted at the stadium run by the Haryana sports department.[35]

---

[33]Baparnash, Tridib. 'Training with Long-Distance Runners Helped Neeraj Chopra Gain Strength, Says Childhood Coach Naseem Ahmad', *The Times of India*, 9 August 2021, https://timesofindia.indiatimes.com/sports/tokyo-olympics/india-in-tokyo/training-with-long-distance-runners-helped-neeraj-chopra-gain-strength-says-childhood-coach-naseem-ahmad/articleshow/85169902.cms. Accessed on 29 November 2021.
[34]Ibid.
[35]Gupta, Shalini. 'Olympic Gold Medallist Neeraj Chopra Has

But it is not an easy task to become a successful sportsman.

Facing the Challenges

No matter how glorious these achievements seem with money and fame, it happens to only a fortunate few. These are the few who have outdone themselves to slice the air with their javelins.

A sportsperson's life is full of immense uncertainty and challenges. Quite often, it starts with parents demotivating their children from taking up a sport. A common couplet that has set the early mindset of students is, '*Padhoge, likhoge toh banoge nawab; kheloge, koodoge toh hoge kharaab* (If you write and read, you'll end up becoming a nawab; if you only play sports, you'll make for a bad example).' This has usually set the early foundation of a youngster's view of sports in India.

The country has a tradition of physical education/training classes, NCC and other physical activities as part of curriculum. But, very often that time is taken up by mathematics or science teachers to finish the classes. The physical teacher/sports trainer in schools ends up doing proctorial duties.

Chandigarh Connect', *Hindustan Times*, 8 August 2021, https://www.hindustantimes.com/cities/chandigarh-news/olympic-gold-medalist-neeraj-chopra-has-chandigarh-connect-101628365146284.html. Accessed on 29 November 2021.

This is the case where schools are rich enough to have physical education teachers. In less elite institutions, the priority stays the same with all but physical education/sports. Hence, a young boy or girl is not trained for sports. Further, much has changed due to the onset of internet, digital platforms and video games. So engaged are the youngsters on their screens that hardly are they seen on sports grounds.

༄

In villages, however, there is hope. It is here that a young one who otherwise toils and supports the family in the fields can potentially utilize his/her natural talent to excel in sports. But what is individual motivation?

I asked the same question to multiple people while researching for this book. What motivates a young sportsman? Take a young boy who has no idea, educate him early on of the work he needs to put in. What will he earn after all the effort he puts in? Quite frankly, there are many answers and varying opinions, and mostly, it is a mix of different things.

First and foremost is the role played by parents. If the parents or one of them is or has been a sportsperson, they usually try hard to inculcate the habit of playing sports. Then comes the role of teachers who have learnt about the impact of sports by way of experience in their lives. These two sets of people play an immense role in deciding if the child will take up sports. Quite often, a child may be very good at sports but it takes immense courage for his guardians to take that leap.

The selection of the sport depends on what parents have played or which sports facilities are available in the immediate vicinity. This is apart from what the child is naturally good at. There is also an essential factor, commonly addressed as a 'fad'. For example, cricket, football or basketball are glitzy games. They have a charm associated with them. People in cities like the glamour associated with it and the young ones in Tier-2, Tier-3 towns aspire for it.

Then there is the financial factor. Delhi Golf Club membership runs into lakhs of rupees, but one could be a regular in wrestling, and dangal circuits for a few hundred. Both games are challenging in their ways, but only someone with the means has access to a golf club. Then, there are the returns on investment. Investing six years of your life in cricket and being good at it could land you a spot in the Ranji Trophy team and even an IPL deal if you do well. Even if you are not exceptional, cricketing circuits are full of sponsorships and advertisements, and the prize money associated with it is good encouragement too. Thanks to other recent sporting events such as Pro Kabaddi, a change is setting in following the IPL success, but more needs to be done.

Then the politics of making it through is another challenge. Said somebody who has done well due to his sporting success, '*Ek gaaon ka ladka aataa hai mere paas guidance ke liye. Main kabhi nahiin kehta team event khelo. Individual khelo. Apne aapko outperform karo. Dekho har gaaon se gold niklega*! (When a boy from a village comes to me for guidance, I never suggest to play at a team event, but individually. Try outperforming yourself. Then watch how every village throws up a gold medal winner).'

That is a very interesting take too. Cricket is a heavily politicized event (hint: Lalit Modi). For anyone to do well in cricket, apart from being very good at the game it is important to know some people and have the right connections, coaches and network.

In the 2017 movie *Mukkabaaz*, Bhojpuri-Bollywood actor Ravi Kissan who plays the role of a boxing coach says, '*Zyada important hai tum kisko jaante ho, kisko pehchante ho; kaun tumko jaantaa hai kaun tumko maantaa hai* (What is more important is who you know, who you recognize; who knows you and who acknowledges you).' This has become the story of so many sportspersons in India.

However, from where does this politicization come? The Indian sporting system works very much on the Gurukul Parampara—the trainer/coach is everything. It is the experience and connections of the coaches which takes one forward. Added to it are the sports federations which themselves have become immensely politicized. Prominent young politicians start or become part of top federations. It helps them connect with the younger sporting generation and participate in numerous public sports events thus increasing their outreach.

Further, the sporting umbrella has numerous vacancies and the politician's clout increases when he obliges some of his men for a job. Similarly, there are coaches, physiotherapists, nutritionists, suppliers and contractors of all kinds who are all related to each other in this mesh.

I am not discounting the good work done by any of them because whoever you ask has a complaint to share. Somebody has always been wronged and someone always has taken this 'system' in his hand and ruled the roost. And then some have risen against the system!

The Uncles

Credit also goes to Neeraj's uncles who knew nothing about the game but trusted the youngster. His friends had become an extension of his family, and to them, he was a younger brother. Friends had started visiting Khandra and the uncles had built up a healthy relationship with all of them.

It was quite an exciting phase in the life of Saab, Sunny and others from the group. Saab was selected for the nursery, and with some coaxing and convincing, Neeraj joined him in Panchkula. This must have been in the middle of 2011, recollected Saab when he went to receive Narender at the stadium gate with Neeraj. The trio was ready with many others in the lively and vibrant training school in Panchkula. This is where the transformation began.

At the time of joining the sports nursery, Neeraj was

barely into his teens. At the age of 13, with javelin training of a few months he threw the implement at nearly 45 m. The sport had started gaining his hold on him. Like he said: '*Dheere-Dheere karta gaya. Achcha lagtaa rahaa. Aur passion se ban gaya ki is aur improve karna hai* (Little by little I kept doing it. It felt better every time. And with passion, I got better and realized that I had to improve).'

Although away from home now, he was never out of sight in those formative years. The family took regular updates from friends and even made surprise visits. Bhim Chopra recollects that there had been many times that he hopped onto a bike or borrowed someone's car. He would wait outside to check if Neeraj was on time on the track and sincere in his efforts.

Bhim also got famous amongst Neeraj's peers at the nursery. He remembers fondly how one day he drove a small red car to the training stadium. He parked his car outside and slept in the car. He had done his bit to observe if Neeraj had been on time. However, he could not escape the others in the camp. And, it was sweetly laughed over by the uncle and nephew.

Role of Ministry and Administration

The SAI is the apex organization working for the development of sports in India. Established in 1982 by the Ministry of Youth Affairs and Sports, SAI works out of its head office in Jawaharlal Nehru Stadium, New Delhi.

Simply put, the SAI sits at the top of all big sporting infrastructure and facilities in the country.

It has two sports academic institutions (Netaji Subhas National Institute of Sports at Patiala, Punjab, and Lakshmibai National College of Physical Education at Thiruvananthapuram in Kerala) that provide certificate courses to PhDs. Then there are 11 Regional Centres (SRCs) spread across India. Regionally, the SRC Chandigarh and the SAI Chaudhary Devi Lal Northern Regional Centre, Sonepat, Haryana, are particularly important.

Apart from that, SAI runs 14 Centres of Excellence (COE/COX), 56 sports training centres and 20 special area games. In addition, the SAI also manages Netaji Subhash High Altitude Training Centre and five stadiums in Delhi. In Haryana, there are COX in Sonipat and Hisar, which are of particular importance. The centres have been at the forefront of significant sporting glories from the region.

Athletics Federation of India

Since javelin is a track and field event in athletics, it is vital to highlight the role of the Athletics Federation of India (AFI). The AFI, as described on its official website 'is the apex body for running and managing athletics in India and is affiliated with World Athletics, the Asian Athletics Association (AAA) and Indian Olympic Association (IOA). The AFI has as many as 32 affiliated state units and institutional units. The AFI came into existence in 1946,

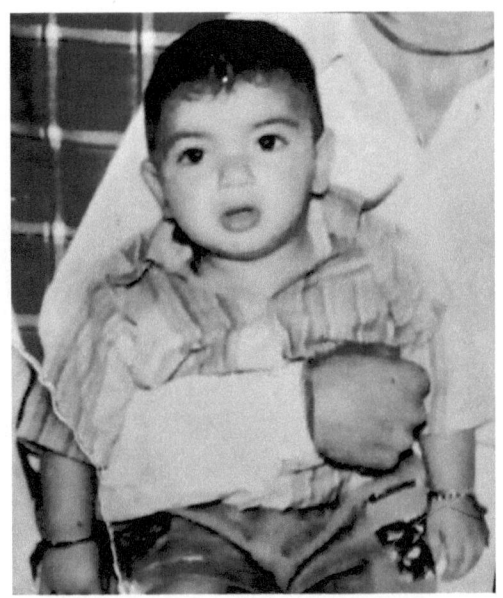

'Chubby' beginnings: Neeraj as a toddler in the late '90s.

Photo courtesy: Surender Chopra

A young Neeraj during his formative years.

Photo courtesy: Surender Chopra

Training to be an Olympic champion: Neeraj (second from right) is seen with (from left) javelin throwers Suman Devi and Annu Rani, Commonwealth Games medallist and former Indian team javelin throw coach Kashinath Naik and javelin thrower, Davinder Singh Kang.

Photo courtesy: Kashinath Naik

Celebrating the gold and the world record: Neeraj poses with his coach Jitender Jaglan (coach Jitu) at a dhaba near Panipat, after his gold-medal winning performance at the IAAF World U-20 Championships in 2016.

Photo courtesy: Jitender Jaglan

Neeraj in action during the 22nd Asian Athletics Championships at the Kalinga Stadium in Bhubaneswar, Odisha, in 2017.

Photo courtesy: Wikimedia Common/Athletics Federation of India

Bonding with fellow athletes at the Tau Devi Lal Stadium, Panchkula. (Clockwise from top right): Parvinder Choudhary, Neeraj, Montu and Paralympian Narender Ranbir.

Photo courtesy: Parvinder Choudhary

The habit of winning: Neeraj Chopra wins gold, while Ahmed B.A. (left) of Qatar and Davinder Singh of India win silver and bronze, respectively, in men's javelin at the 22nd Asian Athletics Championships in Bhubaneswar, Odisha, in 2017.

Photo courtesy: Wikimedia Commons/Athletics Federation of India

Neeraj being felicitated by officials after his spectacular performance at the 22nd Asian Athletics Championships in Bhubaneswar, Odisha, in 2017.

Photo courtesy: Wikimedia Commons/Athletics Federation of India

Recognition for outstanding performance in sports and games: Neeraj receives the Arjuna Award from President Ram Nath Kovind at the Rashtrapati Bhavan in 2018.

Photo courtesy: Wikimedia Common/Office of President of India

Neeraj celebrates his Arjuna Award with his childhood friend, Sunny.

Photo courtesy: Sunny

Union Minister for Information and Broadcasting and Youth Affairs and Sports, Anurag Thakur (third from right), along with Union Minister of Law and Justice, Kiren Rijiju, (second from left) felicitating Tokyo Olympics gold medallist Neeraj Chopra at a function in New Delhi on 9 August 2021. Minister of State for Home Affairs, Youth Affairs and Sports, Nisith Pramanik (on the extreme left), is also seen.

Photo Courtesy: Press Information Bureau, Government of India

Neeraj praying in the family fields in Panipat.
Photo courtesy: Surender Chopra

Proud parents Satish Kumar and Saroj Devi.
Photo courtesy: Surender Chopra

Neeraj with his extended family.

Photo courtesy: Surender Chopra

Jab We Met: Neeraj Chopra meets his biographer, Arjun Singh Kadian, in Panipat in October 2021.

Photo courtesy: Arjun Singh Kadian

and the federation organizes the national and international championships. It trains the Indian athletics national campers, selects the athletics teams for various international competitions, including the Olympics, Asian Games, CWG, World Championships, Asian Championships and other global meets. It also conducts the national and international championships for various age categories.

Besides promoting the sport, the AFI popularizes it amongst the masses and makes athletics commercially attractive for further growth of athletes. The federation also supervises and assists its state units in their activities, plans and sets up special coaching camps, training for coaches and takes initiatives for development programme and grassroot promotion of athletics in India.'[36]

The AFI also has a reputation of bringing back a majority of medals at the Asian Games and has a legacy of stars such as legendary Henry Rebello, 'Flying Sikh' Milkha Singh, the 'Jim Thorpe of India' Gurbachan Singh Randhawa, Sriram Singh, P.T. Usha, World Athletics gold medallist Anju Bobby George, Commonwealth Games Gold medallist Krishna Poonia, two-time Asian Games gold medallist Ashwini Akunji, among others.[37]

The federation and the authority work in tandem to develop athletics in India and make glorious history from

---

[36] Athletics Federation of India, https://indianathletics.in/about-afi/. Accessed on 29 November 2021.
[37] Ibid.

Indian sporting groups. Then there is the flagship scheme of the Prime Minister Narendra Modi-led government—Target Olympic Podium Scheme (TOPS).

Under the prime minister's directions, the sports ministry started TOPS in September 2014 to improve India's performance in the Olympic Games and Paralympic Games. As many as 160 athletes are in the TOPS core group and 259 in TOPS development group.

The direct support to Indian athletes is done under the Annual Calendar for Training and Competition. These are for national camps in India and overseas, including board and lodging, international competitions, salaries to coaches and support staff (both Indian and overseas) and the national competitions by the national sports federations.

TOPS covers nearly everything not provided under the Annual Calendar for Training and Competition, including specialized training and competition, additional coach and support staff fee, purchase of personalized equipment, medical support, and a monthly stipend of ₹50,000 for each athlete (TOPS Core Group) and ₹25,000 (TOPS development group).

Tokyo Olympic medallist weightlifter Mirabai Chanu was funded for her two-and-a-half-month-long rehabilitation and training in St Louis under Dr Aaron Horschig's supervision by TOPS. Similarly, Bajrang Punia, who spent 1,000 days in national camps in India and overseas, trained in Russia just before the Olympic Games.

TOPS funded that and the stay of sparring partners for all the wrestlers.

Neeraj spoke highly of the programme and SAI support earlier in 2021: 'Their (SAI and TOPS) support and financial assistance for equipment, international exposure trips and help to players injured during competition and training is helping us in a big way... They are motivating us to give it our best shot. SAI ensured that athletes could get back to training as quickly as possible after the lockdown and promptly opened the ground and training facilities with COVID-19-compliant protocols.'[38]

Neeraj is also a TOPS athlete, and it funded his six-week competition and training trip entirely to Europe ahead of Tokyo 2020. Coach Dr Klaus Bartonietz and a physiotherapist accompanied him.

What if He Gave Up?

Neeraj was once asked, '*Agar javelin thrower nahin hote toh kya karte life mein?* (Had you not become a javelin thrower, what would you have done in life?)' Neeraj, well aware of his background, laughed and said, '*Kuch nahin karta ji. Gaaon mein bhainson ko dande maarta* (I would not do

---

[38]TOPS and SAI Have Helped Indian Athletes Immensely, Claims Neeraj Chopra', *SportsCafe*, 4 November 2021, https://www.sportscafe.in/sports/articles/2021/apr/11/2021-tokyo-olympics-tops-and-sai-have-helped-indian-athletes-immensely-claims-neeraj-chopra. Accessed on 29 November 2021.

anything. Just beat the buffaloes with my stick).'

And that may well have been the situation. Had Neeraj not been throwing the javelin or doing well in the sport, he would have returned to the village and continued living in oblivion. But the family may not have lost spirit.

The Chopra family had already seen the lows. They were striving hard to get out of their situation and elevate their status. There was no going back. Neeraj had to work hard, just like the rest of the clan. There was no scope of failure, and had he failed, the family would have tried for another opportunity to strike back.

Hence, at the beginning of 2012, Neeraj was in Panchkula, raring to go.

6

Soaring High

'Neeraj is a natural'

—Coach Gary Calvert

As many of Neeraj's peers say, he picked up the sport very quickly. In no time, he had a clear idea of the stance, the turn and the throw. His flexibility was remarkable, and his attitude towards the game was the icing on the cake.

As coach Naseem Ahmad said, 'His fundamentals were strong,' and so he became part of the Panipat performers' chain.[39] Neeraj quickly won district level medals and

---

[39]Sharma, Nitin. 'Former coach recalls chubby Neeraj Chopra with a

caught the eye of good people in the athletics ecosystem. The weight gain in Khandra, those workouts in Madlauda, Panipat, and all the guidance from friends and coaches started paying off quickly.

Lucknow, 2012

Since Independence, the various governments did little to develop sports in India because they were usually slow to get off the blocks. Unlike them, the Uttar Pradesh (UP) government established a sports college in 1975 in Lucknow. With 153 acres of land available, the college has contributed much to the development of sports in the region.[40]

In October 2012, this college became a vibrant hub for budding sportspersons from across India. Both Saab and Neeraj made their way to the 'City of Nawabs'. Lucknow's charm has always attracted people of all hues and colours.

While Saab was representing Haryana in the U-18 category, Neeraj Chopra was doing the honours in U-16. Saab, a confident young man of 17, represented the state with Surender. He threw a gigantic 71.16 m, and was awarded with a bronze medal. The gold and silver medals

---

notebook, now an Olympic gold medallist', *The Indian Express*, 8 August 2021, https://indianexpress.com/article/olympics/former-coach-recalls-the-chubby-kid-with-a-notebook-now-an-olympic-gold-medallist-neeraj-chopra-7443442/. Accessed on December 8 2021.

[40]Guru Gobind Singh Sports College, Lucknow, http://upsports.gov.in/article/sportscollege-en/about-us. Accessed on 29 November 2021.

went to UP's Abhishek Singh and Satyendra Kumar, respectively. It is interesting to note that Abhishek Singh broke the national record of 72.25 m (U-18, 700 g javelin set by Rajesh Kumar in 2011.

However, a bigger magic was on display in the U-16 event. A few months short of 15, Neeraj threw the 700 g Javelin to a distance of 68.46 m—a national record.

Dharmender Kumar Patel set the previous U-16 record in 2007 while the meet record was set in 2005. In those years, nobody could trump the feat, until Neeraj bettered the meet record. He established a new national record of 68.46 m in the afternoon of 27 October 2012. Another player from Haryana, Mandeep Kumar, came second.

At the same event, Rajesh Kumar set the U-20 national record by throwing the javelin to a distance of 80.14 m. This was around eight metres more than the silver medallist, Abhilash. Kumari Sharmila from Haryana also set a new national record of 47.31 m in the U-18 Girls 500 g javelin throw.[41]

Haryanvi javelin throwers had started to make their way onto the national circuit. Breaking records spoke of the progress that the sport and players had been making in the last few years.[42]

---

[41] https://view.officeapps.live.com/op/view.aspx?src=https%3A%2F%2Findianathletics.in%2Fwp-content%2Fresults%2F2012%2Fresults%25202012.xls&wdOrigin=BROWSELINK

[42] Results, Atheletics Federation of India, https://indianathletics.in/results/. Accessed on 29 November 2021.

Neeraj trained in Panckhula from 2011 to somewhere close to 2016. This association to Panchkula raised his game, and he was called for the national camp in Patiala. With performances like this at the junior nationals, Neeraj had finally announced his arrival.

Another event that Neeraj participated in 2012 was an inter-district national championship in Haridwar. He established a new meet record here as well. Neeraj got back to Panchkula and started training again.

40-40-40

The Haryana Festival was a sports event organized in Panchkula. At the end of the festival, Neeraj was fooling around on the basketball court when he tripped and broke his right wrist. The injury was at a very typical place and severe. It took him five to six months to recover.

The wrist was plastered thrice for 40 days each time. The first time the plaster was opened rather quickly, believing that it may have healed, but that was not the case. A repercussion of this was that Neeraj was mainly absent from other competitive events in 2012.

10th National Youth Athletics

On 20 May 2013, the B.R. Stadium in Guntur (Andhra Pradesh) held the 10th National Youth Athletics Championships. Performing in the U-16 category with a 700 g javelin, Neeraj came second with a best throw of 65.68 m. Another Haryana athlete, Mandeep Kumar, a year older than Neeraj, threw 67.02 m. With a silver medal, Neeraj was selected for his first international event.

Mandeep and Neeraj then flew to Ukraine for the World Youth Championships.

Donetsk, 2013

Around a year before the ongoing conflict between Ukraine and Russia-Donbas began, Donetsk hosted athletes from across the world for the World Youth Championships in July 2013.

Neeraj participated in the tournament alongside Mandeep Kumar. None of them, however, could make it to the podium. Neeraj came nineteenth in the qualifying round. But this was his first big international outing. And he was just 15.

What was more important was that the young boy from Khandra who picked up a javelin just two-and-a-half years back was now flying abroad to represent the country. This was a giant leap. Neeraj remembers being excited about it. He had a window seat on the aircraft and reminisced, *'Itna excited they hum, bahar hee dekhte rahe* (I was so excited that I kept looking out).' An even bigger reason for the excitement was that Neeraj received the India kit for the first time. During a discussion Neeraj said, *'Yeh bahaut badaa sapna hota hai..athletes ka...ki India ke liye khelein* (This is a huge dream for any Indian athlete, to play for his country).'

Indeed, it was unreal, but it was all the result of sheer hard work. The fears of injury were in the past now.[43]

ೂ

Neeraj and the senior boys also trained at Madhuban, in Karnal, near the end of 2013. After returning from the World Youth Championships, they took a room near the Namaste Chowk in Karnal and trained there for two to three months. Madhuban has a police academy with good facilities available for sports.

Rajender Singh and 2014

Neeraj had by now turned 16, and that shifted his age category for tournaments. This also meant that he would be competing with other senior players in the game. One such remarkable story from Haryana was that of Rajender Singh.

Rajender Singh is a humble and hard-working man who toils day and night, training rigorously on the grounds of Narwana to improve the lives of young sportspersons there. Narwana is a small town in the Jind district of Haryana.

---

[43]'Shankar, Saurabh. 'Neeraj Chopra: India's Olympic javelin hope', *International Olympic Committee*, 8 December 2019, https://olympics.com/en/featured-news/neeraj-chopra-india-javelin. Accessed on 8 December 2021.

In contemporary times, it had become popular because of some famous electoral battles. However, in those few years, Rajender Singh had become the region's pride thanks to his feats on the national stage.

Rajender was from a family with limited means. There were no facilities available around him. He took it upon himself to repair the ground, remove stone fragments on the run-up strip and level it so that players did not twist their ankles and destroy their careers.

Incidentally, Rajender picked up the sport by accident in late 2004. He used to play cricket and, somehow, thanks to the support of his uncle, it continued. In no time, Rajender went from representing his school to the district and then to state-level competitions. Rajender credited coach Karan Singh for his fundamental training. He said, '*Root lagaane waale aadmi they* (He is the one who strengthened my fundamentals).' Karan Singh saw the potential before Rajender's height would change the latter's fortunes.

In 2005, Rajender shifted base to Hisar. Although javelin was an unpopular sport then, athletes would travel from Bhiwani, a sporting hub in Haryana. However, in 2006, Rajender's fortunes took a hit. It is rather telling of the turmoil our sportsmen have to undergo before they finally make it to the national glory and world stage.

Rajender remembers those days vividly. He trained vigorously for the Federation Cup U-20 Tournament. The training took a toll on his body and he fell ill. Because he had no clue about doping and banned salts, he believed it was best to skip all medicines. Doing so, he thought would save him from all fears. The repercussions were pretty bad. He remained ill for 10 days, followed by immense weakness, and in no time he lost the year. This limited access to medical facilities cost Rajender nearly 18 months.

Rajender picked up the sport again in 2008 and performed well on all fronts—junior nationals, zonal events, etc. In 2009, he created a new state record at the Haryana Open event with a throw of over 72 m. His performance improved by leaps and bounds thereafter. Everyone in those years was doing well in javelin, and there was a healthy competition in place. Throwers were trying to outdo each other while establishing new benchmarks. The only motivation was self-motivation and the spirit, *'Kuch dikhaanaa hai!* (Have to show them what I can do).'

In 2010, Rajender came fourth in the Commonwealth Games. Another player, Kashinath Naik, representing India, won the bronze. Rajender remembers the women's relay team winning the gold as he walked out. That is when it dawned on him that he had let slip a great opportunity.

However, he quickly got back on his feet. He performed well in 2013 and 2014. Along with Davinder Kang, Rajender became an inspiration to young javelin throwers in the day.

At the Senior Federation Cup at NIS Patiala, on 17 August 2014, Rajender set a meet record with a throw of 79.32 m. Davinder was second with 78.57 m. In the same tournament, a young Neeraj Chopra came eighth with a throw of 70.19 m.

Neeraj's performances, however, were way more remarkable in the 700 g javelin events. He set a meet record when he threw 74.76 m at the 26th North Zone competition. At the 11th National Youth Athletics Championship in April 2014, Neeraj delivered a gold medal performance.[44]

His peak performance continued at the 30th National Juniors on 30 November 2014 in Vijayawada (Andhra Pradesh), organized by the Andhra Pradesh Athletics Association. In the afternoon session, wearing a grey T-shirt soaked in sweat, Neeraj wore a lower back brace and elbow support. He was lean, with longish hair and delivered a great throw of 76.50 m, setting a national record.

∽

All this time Neeraj was putting up at the sports nursery in Panchkula. If the nursery was shut, for some reason, he would stay outside on some other arrangements. But for the most time, Panchkula was home.

---

[44]'26th Northzone Athletics Championships-2014', PAC Stadium, Lucknow, https://view.officeapps.live.com/op/view.aspx?src=https%3A%2F%2Findianathletics.in%2Fwp-content%2Fresults%2F2014%2Fresults%25202014.xls&wdOrigin=BROWSELINK. Accessed on 15 December 2021.

Thiruvananthapuram, 2015

In February, the 35th National Games (Athletics) 2015 opened at the University Stadium in Thiruvananthapuram. On the evening of 12 February, the Men's Javelin event began amidst much fanfare. Javelin players had been giving top competitive performances everywhere, raising the overall standard of the game in the country.

Players such as Devender Singh, Vipin Kasana (a top athlete from UP) and Rajinder Singh were ready to perform to their best. Even Neeraj, who had only recently started competing in the senior category, was ready.

Representing Haryana, Neeraj threw a 73.5-m distance. It was, however, Rajinder Singh's day. Standing at 5'8", Rajinder was a muscular man who had the strength of a weightlifter. He released the javelin with all his might. He jumped up and down thrice on the spot, realizing that he had delivered a knock-out punch. The javelin flew high through the air and landed at a distance of 82.23 m. Rajinder was comfortably ahead by two metres of the previous record set by Anil Kumar Singh in 2008.[45]

Davinder came second with 75.34 m and Vipin won Bronze with a throw of 75.18 m.[46] Looking back, Neeraj

---

[45]'National Mark by Rajinder in javelin; Gold for Renjith', *The Telegraph*, 24 November 2021, https://www.telegraphindia.com/sports/national-mark-by-rajinder-nbsp-in-javelin-gold-for-renjith/cid/1481117. Accessed on 29 November 2021.

[46]https://view.officeapps.live.com/op/view.aspx?src=https%3A%2F

knew then that he could outdo this one. He was younger, taller and not bogged down by any serious injuries.

Regardless of his performance in the National Games, he received a call from the National Camp in Patiala. Davinder Singh Kang called Saab and shared that his training partner had been selected for the National Camp. His friends were delighted!

ॐ

Another person who had a role to play in this selection was Rajender Singh. He pursued the officials at the camp, convincing them that the young man had potential. Neeraj was making remarkable progress and showed immense potential. Rajender spoke with chief coach Radhakrishan Iyer and ensured that the boy was given an opportunity at the camp. This also reflected on Rajender's nature. He believed that a young talent such as Neeraj should not go through the kind of troubles he had to endure. Neeraj was selected for the national camp, and it was a game-changer.

Iyer's decision was also based on his assessment. Neeraj had a very fast hand speed of release. He had a word with AFI Planning Commission Chairman Lalit Bhanot and Neeraj joined the national camp.[47]

%2Findianathletics.in%2Fwp-content%2Fresults%2F2015%2Fresults%25202015.xls&wdOrigin=BROWSELINK

[47]PTI. 'It Was Neeraj Chopra's Decision to Part Ways with Uwe Hohn—Athletics Chief Coach', *The Bridge*, 8 August 2021, https://thebridge.in/

Getting Better in 2015

At the camp, Neeraj's performance started to improve swiftly. There were numerous reasons for it. At NIS, the facilities were remarkably better than he had previously received anywhere. Beginning with the very basic thing—the javelin. World-class implements like those of Nordic javelins were available for the athletes. Another thing was nutrition. In Panchkula or elsewhere, the boys, including Neeraj, would cook their food. Toiling through the day, working on their skills, the boys would return to the room tired. '*Daliya banaane ko rakh diya...Neend aayi rehti thi... Bread ke saath daliya kha lena* (We would make daliya and despite how sleep deprived we were, we would have daliya and bread).'

At Panchkula, the boys had no pattern and schedule with regards to their diet. At times they would skip lunches or have a heavy breakfast to not disrupt their training. In the evenings, post-training, they would have some rotis, cook their vegetables and drink milk straight from packets. In a nutshell, this was not the diet a proper athlete should have had. As a result, the boys would put in the hard work, but their body would recover slowly.

In contrast, at the national camp, nutrition was ensured, and food was timely. It had better support staff and seniors.

---

athletics/neeraj-chopra-decision-uwe-hohn-athletics-coach-24304. Accessed on 29 November 2021.

Along with it came the competitive spirit. Neeraj's entire world changed drastically. From now on, the only focus was on improving the throw and achieving distances with the javelin.

Furthermore, Neeraj started to focus more on how his body reacted and responded to different drills and exercises. He began to understand the kind and extent of training that was good for his body.

∽

CWG medal winner of 2010, Kashinath Naik, had stopped participating in competitive javelin events after a while. From 2013 to 2018, he was the national coach for javelin and contributed to improving Neeraj's game. Naik began coaching Neeraj but in a few weeks, Neeraj and he parted ways—Naik's schedules were not suiting him. It was strenuous and Neeraj found it challenging to get used to it.

At the camp, Neeraj had left his old Panipat group behind. He was, of course, still in touch with them and reached out to Monu whenever he needed, but he was a lone warrior now. He would exercise, drill and train alone. It was now consultations with seniors at the camp which helped him elevate his game. The results started to show quickly.

Neeraj bettered himself in May 2015 when he created a national meet record of 76.91 m. Mayank won the second position, coming in seven metres behind Neeraj.

Neeraj delivered another excellent performance at the 19th National Federation Cup Senior Athletics Championships, 2015 at Mangaluru (Karnataka). He hit the 73.96-m mark and came second to Davinder Singh who threw 79.65 m. In August, Neeraj threw 77.37 m, winning the gold at the 55th National Interstate Athletics Championships in Chennai (Tamil Nadu). In September the same year, Neeraj inched closer to the 80-m mark when he threw 77.67 m at the 55th National Open athletics championships 2015 at the SAI Centre, Kolkata (West Bengal).[48]

∽

At the Punjab University Athletics Meet in Chandigarh in November, Neeraj dazzled with a meet record of 76.66 m, but the best was round the corner. During the All Inter-University Games of 2015, Neeraj delivered his best performance so far. He had turned 18 only a week back and delivered his first 80-m throw.

It is important to note that after passing ninth class at B.V.N. School, Neeraj continued his studies through the open education pattern. That is usually the way followed by excelling sportspersons. He then took admission at the DAV School, Chandigarh, in 2015. The education, however,

---

[48] https://view.officeapps.live.com/op/view.aspx?src=https%3A%2F%2Findianathletics.in%2Fwp-content%2Fresults%2F2015%2Fresults%25202015.xls&wdOrigin=BROWSELINK

was constantly disrupted due to his competitions. For example, his examinations were scheduled around the SAF Games (now called the South Asian Games). He had to skip them because his focus was on the competitions and consequently the Olympics.

12th South Asian Games (Athletics), 2016

The South Asian Games is a multi-sport event which is the regional games of the Olympic Council of Asia. Barring a few occasions, it had been held regularly since being hosted first in Kathmandu, Nepal, in 1984. The 12th South Asian Games started on 5 February 2016, in Guwahati, Assam. Prime Minister Narendra Modi opened the event. India saw a record medal haul—308 out of total 789. The theme song 'Ei Prthibi Ek Krirangan' by Bhupen Hazarika set the tone for a wonderful event.

Athletes from India, Pakistan, Sri Lanka, Bangladesh and Nepal participated in the event. While Arshad Nadeem led the Pakistan contingent, Neeraj Chopra and Samarjit Singh Malhi spearheaded the Indian squad. Neeraj who had recently crossed the 80-m mark, delivered a wonderful performance winning the gold with his personal best throw of 82.23 m. That equalled Rajinder Singh's national record.[49]

---

[49]Chopra Nails World Junior Record to Win Javelin Gold', *Deccan Herald*, 24 July 2016, https://www.deccanherald.com/content/559777/chopra-nails-world-junior-record.html. Accessed on 29 November 2021.

The Indian Express wrote: 'In ten strides, the six-foot 90-kilogram athlete sprints close to his peak velocity. Still accelerating, his right heel rotates sideways as he cross strides. His upper body rotates clockwise as he approaches the throwing mark, building torque like a wound-up spring. His javelin bearing arm is slowly extended away from his torso. Coiled and now cocked, his left leg braces hard just ahead of the foul line. His body swings over like a door on its hinge sending the projectile hurtling towards the other end of the stadium away from his scream of exertion. The sharpened tip buries into the turf 82.23 m away.'[50]

ೲ

Another legendary sportsman at the NIS Patiala Campus, Garry Calvert, was watching his performance. Australian by origin, Calvert had recently arrived in Patiala as India's javelin coach. Watching Neeraj on his flickering television screen, he knew he was watching a star in the making.

Calvert was an expert in the rotational technique of the javelin throw. He had trained the likes of Mitchell Johnson, the Australian pace bowler, before the latter took up cricket as a sport. Another star performer was Jarrod Bannister,

---

[50] Selvaraj, Jonathan. 'India's Latest Athletics Sensation Neeraj Chopra Is Brimming with Natural Talent', *The Indian Express*, 28 February 2016, https://indianexpress.com/article/sports/sport-others/neeraj-chopra-javelin-south-asian-games-garry-calvert/. Accessed on 29 November 2021.

who threw 89.02 m in 2008.[51] Owing to his differences with Indian sports authorities with regards to an extension of his contract, Calvert quit the Indian team a little over a year later and took the Chinese offer after considering the other few he had. However, he suffered a heart attack and died in July 2018.

Many stories of his kindness poured from all over. Neeraj who was then training in Finland, tweeted, 'Very saddened to hear about the demise of coach Gary Calvert, who died of a heart attack yesterday. I had done a lot of hard work under him in 2016–17 and got to learn a lot. You were a good friend and coach. You will always be remembered. RIP'[52]

Calvert's contribution to Neeraj's sport was indelible as he added another four metres to his throw. Calvert was highly impressed by Neeraj's fundamentals and mechanics of his throw. Javelin throw is actually about getting the longest movement of the throw in the shortest time. An arm delay generates this long movement.

Calvert would say, 'Most throwers in an attempt to throw the javelin as quickly as possible, don't draw their throwing arm as far as they could. The longer they delay

---

[51]Ibid.
[52]Amsan, Andrew. 'Garry Calvert, The Gentle Soul Who Shaped Neeraj Chopra's Career, Passes Away at 63', *The Indian Express*, 29 July 2018, https://indianexpress.com/article/sports/sport-others/garry-calvert-the-gentle-soul-who-shaped-neeraj-chopras-career-no-more-5281111/. Accessed on 29 November 2021.

releasing their arm, the more distance they can get. Arm delay is something, you keep trying to drill into an athletes head. Today, perhaps just the best five throwers have that quality. (Jarrod) Bannister had it but it took 12 years for him to get to that stage. Neeraj already has that ability.'

Calvert was impressed with Neeraj from the early days. He said, 'He is someone you can watch throw all day. You can look at a 1,000 javelin throwers and suddenly along comes this boy who understands delay. Even though he is a junior, and sometimes I can't believe that, Neeraj just stands out amongst his competition.'[53]

With Calvert, Neeraj attended many camps in Bangalore and outside India. Calvert was not particularly happy with the facilities available in India. But what worked for Neeraj was his non-conflicting nature. He would insist that his only focus was on improving his performance and staying away from politics of the federations and other stakeholders. Hence, SAI, AFI, JSW and coaches, all converged to help Neeraj grow. Funds and support for these foreign camps came from the AFI and SAI. Neeraj would also compete more frequently abroad and get the necessary exposure.

∽

---

[53]Selvaraj, Jonathan. 'India's Latest Athletics Sensation Neeraj Chopra Is Brimming with Natural Talent', *The Indian Express*, 28 February 2016, https://indianexpress.com/article/sports/sport-others/neeraj-chopra-javelin-south-asian-games-garry-calvert/. Accessed on 29 November 2021.

The improvement at the national camp was rather remarkable. In its initial phase, he was guided by Kashinath Naik. However, he dropped Naik as he had problems with his drills.[54] This speaks of another laudable attribute of the sportsman. Neeraj knew what he wanted and what would help him give his best performance. He ensured that he stuck to what worked for him and quickly moved away from things that did not.

Quite often and during research for the book, I spoke to sportspersons who confided in me that since the federation and association had brought an expensive foreign coach for them, they felt they had to be with him, or it would make the federation look bad. They would add that it was only after they lost out on a medal, did they realize that that might not be the way forward.

Neeraj did this with Naik and even skipped a few workouts with Baba Coach. His reasons were simple—if something helps me, I will include it in my training. If it did not, I would stop it quickly.[55]

What made Neeraj stand out was that he was an extremely humble guy who was ever eager to ask for suggestions. He would ask other players, even from among his competitors, to spot mistakes in his technique. For example, he credits Rajinder Singh for pointing out that Neeraj's right leg was too wide during the crossover phase,

---

[54]Ibid.
[55]Ibid.

which resulted in lesser power.[56] And, of course, there was YouTube!

Neeraj would learn better techniques and drills from YouTube. It could be risky because he could be doing something incorrectly and not be aware of it. In 2015 and 2016, he showed constant improvement, so one can assume that he was probably doing the right thing.

Another notable thing at this point was his fitness level. Nearly all other players, friends and fellow trainers had by now started losing out to some injury. Neeraj, on the other hand, felt only some physical pain during the inter-university event in Patiala. But it was all seemingly good. His body, observed Donavan Pillai, bio kineticist for Kwa-Zulu Natal Dolphins Cricket Union, seemed to be designed for javelin.[57]

༄

Another notable performance in 2016 was at the Indian Grand Prix at Jawaharlal Nehru Stadium, New Delhi, in April. Neeraj won the gold while Shivpal Singh, who is now in the Indian Air Force, won the silver medal.

JSW

The Jindal family, originally from Hisar, Haryana, is a business conglomerate today with interests in minerals,

---

[56]Ibid.
[57]Ibid.

energy, etc. JSW Sports is the sporting arm of the JSW Group, a $13 billion conglomerate. 'Established in 2012, the company aims to play a leading role in creating a sporting culture in India by maximizing the potential of Indian sports and athletes.'[58] In a short span, the organization had earned many laurels and given wings to many sporting sensations in the country. As a consequence of these efforts, it was awarded the Khel Protsahan Puruskar in 2018. It was also honoured with the FICCI Sports Award 2018 for being the Best Company Promoting Sports (Private Sector).

The organization supported Indian athletes by providing them with the means outside the traditional ecosystem, empowering Indian sports in these dynamic times. It also established the Inspire Institute of Sports in Vijayanagar, Karnataka. It was India's first 'privately-funded High Performance Training Centre that trained talented young athletes across five Olympic disciplines—wrestling, boxing, judo, athletics and swimming. Spread over 42 acres in Vijayanagar, Karnataka, IIS was a unique initiative led by the group. It brought together 23 corporate donors who were collectively funding the operations of the institute through Corporate Social Responsibility funding.'[59]

The conversation and discussion with JSW began soon

---

[58] JSW Sports, https://www.jsw.in/sports/about-jsw-sports. Accessed on 29 November 2021.

[59] JSW, Inspire Institute of Sport, https://www.jsw.in/sports/inspire-institute-sport/. Accessed on 29 November 2021.

after the gold medal performance in Chennai. CWG gold medallist of 2010, boxer Manoj Kumar shared the contact details of Ramdhari Yadav. Manoj said, '*Tera mann kare toh inse baat karke dekh lena for sponsor* (You can call him up if you need a sponsor).' Getting a sponsor was another benchmark every athlete hoped to cross early in his/her sporting career. Playing any sport in India is challenging. There is a serious shortage of world-class facilities, and whatever is available is very expensive and mainly out of reach for most sportspersons.

Hence, Neeraj was on the lookout for a sponsor and JSW sounded interested. Reminding that the senior national opens were round the corner, Yadav suggested, 'Let us look at the performance there, and accordingly, we shall see.' This was in August–September 2015. After that, JSW joined Neeraj's journey.[60]

In those early days with JSW, Neeraj's requirements from the sponsor were not much. He was happy with the facilities at the national camp. JSW gave Neeraj monthly support of around ₹12,000 to ₹13,000 along with supplements and other things.

After his performance at the World juniors, JSW also felt that Neeraj had potential and could reach out for whatever he needed. Neeraj would stay in touch with Yadav

---

[60]'My Mission Is to Put the Tricolor on the Podium', JSW Sports, https://www.jsw.in/sports/jsw-sports-interviews-neeraj-chopra. Accessed on 29 November 2021.

for his requirements. This, however, was scaled up only after Neeraj's performance at the World Juniors.

JSW became a more concrete partner in Neeraj's journey after an inter-university medal and the SAF Games win. In fact, after his gold medal-winning performance in the SAF Games, Neeraj joined JSW's Olympic programme. After his U-20 championships, JSW attached a manager to Neeraj to facilitate his brand management such as Gatorade. Thus, in more ways than one, 2015 became a year of watershed moment in Neeraj's life.

2016 World U-20 Athletics Championships

In July 2016, young athletes (born no earlier than 1 January 1997) assembled in Poland for the 2016 World U-20 championships in athletics. The event was previously called World Junior Championships in Athletics.

Bydgoszcz, also known as Little Berlin, is a city in northern Poland full of architecturally rich structures. In the early medieval ages, the town was an important settlement. It became a hub for athletes for the event organized between 19 and 24 July 2016. A total of 1,359 athletes participated in 44 events at the Zdzisław Krzyszkowiak Stadium there. Neeraj was then training in Spala (in Poland) and drove down to the venue with no visa hiccups.

Neeraj created history there by becoming the first Indian athlete to become a world champion. He won the gold medal by throwing his javelin to a distance of 86.48 m. The previous record of 84.69 m was held by Latvian Zigismunds Sirmais. In the process, Neeraj also established a new national record. What took Rajender Singh innumerable disappointments to set, was shattered by this U-20 lad from Khandra. The village was making its presence marked overseas. 'Sarpanchji' had arrived! Date: 23 July 2016.

Neeraj said, 'When the spear left my hand on that second throw, I had a feeling that this was a special throw. I don't think I expected it to go over 86 m. For the last couple of months, I have worked hard on my fitness, my technique, and it all paid off today.'

The improvement in his performances had been remarkable—70.19 m in 2014, 81.04 m in 2015 and this throw of 86.48 m in 2016. It was astronomical!

However, Neeraj narrowly missed out on an Olympic berth. The 2016 Summer Olympics were in Rio de Janeiro, Brazil. While Neeraj achieved the remarkable feat on 23 July, the deadline to qualify for the Olympics ended on 11 July. Neeraj had the target in his mind, but a minor back injury in April hampered those plans.[61]

---

[61]Selvaraj, Jonathan. 'Neeraj Chopra Creates History to Become First Indian World Champion in Athletics', *The Indian Express*, 24 July 2016, https://indianexpress.com/article/sports/sport-others/neeraj-chopra-creates-history-becomes-first-indian-world-champion-in-athletics-2932114/. Accessed on 29 November 2021.

Rio Olympics, 2016

The Games of the XXXI Olympiad or the 2016 Summer Olympics were held in August 2016. India entered the event with high hopes, riding on the London Olympics wave.

London 2012 proved to be historic from India's perspective, with a contingent of 83 athletes bringing home six Olympic medals—two silver and four bronze. The tally count included Shooting (two), wrestling (two), boxing (one) and badminton (one). London taught everyone that imagining India as a sporting nation was not a distant dream anymore. It was something to strive for!

Shooter Gagan Narang could not sleep properly for a couple of days after winning the bronze medal in the Men's 10 m air rifle.[62] Similarly, M.C. Mary Kom's bronze changed her life, bringing her massive recognition.[63] These performances set the bar high for the 2016 Rio Olympics. Enthusiasts, specifically from Badminton, Shooting, Wrestling and Boxing were looking forward to the Gold Quest in 2016.

An anticipating nation was eagerly looking forward to experiencing individual victories and joy through the

---

[62]Pitts, Andre. 'How Gagan Narang Buried Beijing Demons at London 2012', *Olympics*, 29 July 2020, https://olympics.com/en/featured-news/indian-shooter-gagan-narang-2012-london-olympics-who-bronze-medal. Accessed on 29 November 2021.

[63]Ganguly, Sudipto. 'India's Mary Kom Basks in Boxing Bronze', *Reuters*, 25 September 2012, https://www.reuters.com/article/uk-boxing-india-marykom-idUKBRE88O0CN20120925. Accessed on 29 November 2021.

athletes. Indians and their connection to the athletes, especially at the Olympics, is wholesomely different. London 2012 was the precursor for Rio 2016, and all Indians were on board to celebrate each athlete.

But looking back, Rio was an affair for Indian heroines. India won two medals—bronze and silver, both by women athletes. Shuttler P.V. Sindhu won silver and wrestler Sakshi Malik won bronze. Malik was born in Mokhra village in Rohtak, Haryana, to father Sukhbir and mother Sudesh Malik. The family had limited means, but she fought her way to glory.

With wrestler Vinesh Phogat being stretchered off the arena, another Haryanvi hope was dashed. In her last eight bout against China's Sun Yanan, Phogat injured her knee and could barely move.[64]

On the other hand, P.V. Sindhu[65], then 21, became the youngest Indian to win a silver Olympic medal and wrote her name in India's sporting history. Sindhu was the second Indian shuttler to win an Olympic medal on her debut at the Olympics.

Previous Olympic medallist Saina Nehwal exited in the

---

[64]Peter, Naveen. 'Rio 2016 Pain Keeps Grappler Vinesh Phogat on Her Toes', *Olympics*, 16 August 2020, https://olympics.com/en/featured-news/indian-wrestler-vinesh-phogat-rio-olympics-2016-knee-injury-quarterfinal-bout. Accessed on 29 November 2021.

[65]'P.V. Sindhu's Olympics Debut and a Life-Changing Silver Medal', Olympics, 17 August 2020, https://olympics.com/en/news/indian-badminton-pv-sindhu-olympics-rio-2016-silver-medal-carolina-marin. Accessed on 29 November 2021.

group round, disappointing many. Consequently, all hopes for a Badminton medal were on Sindhu. And she did not disappoint. In an *India Today* exclusive, Sindhu said, 'I've done it' and added 'Overall I am on cloud nine, it was amazing, I was very well prepared. In a match, one wins and one loses, today Marin won.'[66]

But the overall performance was rather dismal despite India sending its largest contingent ever. The contingent had world champions, Olympic medallists, Asian Games medallist, CWG medallists who aced their respective Games, making their entry into Rio 2016. But it was an opportunity missed.

While Sakshi Malik and P.V. Sindhu shone in their debut and bagged medals, there were athletes whose stars did not align and who missed the podium finish and the opportunity of seeing medals in their name.

For instance, there was Dipa Karmakar.[67] Dipa's victory could have transformed the fate of Indian gymnastics. She missed out on a bronze by just 0.15 points. Dipa's story was

---

[66]*India Today* Exclusive: I've Done It, Says PV Sindhu after Rio Silver', *India Today*, 20 August 2016, https://www.indiatoday.in/rio-olympics-2016/india-olympics/story/india-today-exclusive-pv-sindhu-rio-2016-336164-2016-08-19. Accessed on 29 November 2021.

[67]Jain, Anshul. 'India at 2016 Rio Olympics Recap: From Historic Badminton Silver to Missing Historic Gymnast Medal', *The Times of India*, 16 July 2021, https://timesofindia.indiatimes.com/sports/tokyo-olympics/india-in-tokyo/india-at-2016-rio-olympics-recap-from-historic-badminton-silver-to-missing-historic-gymnastics-medal/articleshow/84467797.cms. Accessed on 29 November 2021.

nothing short of a baggage of hardships that she had faced during her training period. She had worked with outdated equipment and apparatus made from piles of crash mats and discarded parts of scooters, but that did not stop her determination and love for gymnastics, leading her to attempt the high-risk Produnova vault.

Dipa's perfectly executed Produnova, made her only the fifth female gymnast in history to do so but could only fetch her fourth place in the table, losing the bronze medal to Guilia Steingruber of Switzerland.[68]

The difference still haunts her, but her performance was the start of something big in the field of gymnastics. To Reuters, she said, 'I want to inspire the next generation so that in 10 to 15 years, India can send a full gymnastics team to an Olympics and not just one athlete.'[69]

Similarly, Kidambi Srikanth,[70] an eminent shuttler from the Gopichand Badminton Academy lost a medal. Sania

---

[68]'India at Olympics 2016: Women Do the Nation Proud at Rio', Olympics, 1 June 2020, https://olympics.com/en/featured-news/india-rio-2016-olympics-medals-pv-sindhu-sakshi-malik. Accessed on 29 November 2021.

[69]Sarkar, Pritha. 'Interview—One Small Step for Dipa Karmakar Could Be a Giant Leap for India', Reuters, 19 August 2016, www.reuters.com/article/olympics-rio-dipakarmakar-interview-idINKCN10U0AR?edition-redirect=in. Accessed on 29 November 2021.

[70]'India at Olympics 2016: Women Do the Nation Proud at Rio', Olympics, 1 June 2020, https://olympics.com/en/featured-news/india-rio-2016-olympics-medals-pv-sindhu-sakshi-malik. Accessed on 29 November 2021.

Mirza and Rohan Bopanna[71] were other hopefuls who failed to shine. Another athlete, Vikas Krishnan, a boxer from Bhiwani, inspired by Vijender Singh's 2008 Beijing performance returned disappointed.

The Indian contingent was full of many known and promising faces such as Abhinav Bindra, Jwala Gutta, Yogeshwar Dutt and others, but it was heartbreaking to see them come back empty-handed.

Javelin@Rio

In Javelin, German Thomas Rohler won the gold medal with a 90.3-m throw. Julius Yego came second and Keshorn Walcott won the bronze with a throw of 85.38 m. Neeraj's throw was a comfortable metre ahead of this bronze performance. Needless to say, he was a little disheartened. Furthermore, there was no representation from India for javelin throw at the Games.

---

[71]Ibid.

7

To the Olympics

In The Army Now

Neeraj's performance at the South Asian Games had attracted all the proper attention. A record performance at the U-20 World Championship followed. Seeing what he had achieved thus far and his potential, the Indian Army offered him a job.

In July 2016, a senior officer of the Army Sports Control Board confirmed that the Army was inducting Neeraj as a Junior Commissioned Officer (JCO) on the post of Naib Subedar. Usually, the Army selects sportspersons as Non-Commissioned officers (NCO) but Neeraj received a JCO rank.

Another step, however, was cleared when Neeraj was finalizing his joining—the young man was to get all the time he needed for training. Neeraj was performing well, and he had to concentrate on one thing alone—the upcoming competitions. Therefore, as soon as he joined, he was sent on an extended leave to continue his training.

The job had a significant role, psychologically speaking. It did what it was supposed to do—act as a backup option. An athlete's life was full of uncertainties and injury fears, ask Monu or Parvinder [Saab's original name]. One had to be very cautious. One never knew when an unexpected injury would curtail a glorious career.

Furthermore, many athletes chose to do this. Some joined the railways or other departments, but the most sought-after placement was in the Services. It added another feather of national pride that a *fauji* had won a medal on the international stage.

Coach Garry Leaves

In April–May 2017, Coach Garry Calvert decided to leave India. Under Calvert's mentorship, Neeraj had outperformed himself during the U-20 World Championship. He was a lovable coach who gave all his support to the players. However, a contractual crisis with SAI made it challenging for him to continue.

The crux of the matter was that Calvert wanted to work with Indian javelin throwers until the Tokyo Olympics. His contract, however, ended in February 2018. Hence, since September 2017, he had been trying to speak to officials to provide him with clarity on his future.

'Resigning midway through a contract with the Asian Athletics Championships just a few months away (in July) and the World Championships later this year, he has been unprofessional as the athletes have been left in the lurch so close to two big events. The Sports Authority of India (SAI) would have looked at giving him a new contract based on the performance of athletes at the World Championships. He had an ongoing contract and by resigning he has violated the contractual obligations,' a top sports ministry official told *The Indian Express*.[72]

Calvert, however, was certain after he met SAI Director General Injeti Srinivas in September. Subsequently, he was asked to approach the Athletics Federation of India, and he forwarded his request for a new contract through them. He spoke with President Adille Sumariwala, Secretary C.K. Valson and Lalit Bhanot. They were all dismissive when he came to them about a new contract. This uncertainty continued since September, and without any assurances, he put in his papers.[73]

---

[72]'Garry Calvert Says SAI Dismissive, SAI Retorts He Was Unprofessional', *The Indian Express*, 11 April 2017, https://indianexpress.com/article/sports/sport-others/garry-calvert-says-sai-dismissive-sai-retorts-he-was-unprofessional-india-javelin-coach-4608095/. Accessed on 29 November 2021.
[73]Ibid.

This added to considerable uncertainty as two big championships were less than four months away. A training and competition trip was on the anvil with Calvert in the run-up to the Asian championships. But to no avail. Calvert also believed that he was one of the lowest paid foreign coaches and should be valued by the federations.

Notably, Calvert had shifted the base of six athletes, including Neeraj, to Bangalore where the climate was much more moderate compared to Patiala winters. Calvert said SAI was dismissive, and SAI responded by calling the Australian unprofessional!

Diamond League, July 2017, Paris

'Bada zabardast, zabardast, zabardast'

—This was Neeraj's reaction when I asked him how the Diamond League experience was.

The Diamond League is an annual series of elite track and field competitions that brings together the best performing athletes for 14 invitational athletics meetings. It is a top-tier event of the World Athletics (previously IAAF) with the inaugural season in 2010. These meetings are all held in the northern hemisphere in the spring and the summer months, in line with the traditional track and field season.

In 2017, invitational meets were held in Oslo, Doha, Shanghai, Rome, Eugene, Lausanne, Fontvieille, London,

Gateshead, Paris, Zurich, Brussels, Stockholm and Rabat. At multiple locations, athletes competed with each other and earned points based on their performance. These points qualified them for the event final held either in Zurich or Brussels. In the case of javelin, the first Diamond League event that Neeraj attended was conducted in Paris and officially named 'Meeting De Paris'.

The competition took place on 1 July 2017, late in the evening, at around 8.30 p.m. The glitzy line-up included Johannes Vetter who won the gold with a throw of 88.74 m. Jakub Vadlech from Czechoslovakia gave a personal best of 88.02 m to come a close second. Other players included Thomas Rohler, Ter Pitkamaki, Magnus Kirt among others. Neeraj, who was the youngest competitor, finished fifth with a throw of 84.67 m.[74]

Notably, his competitors were the very best in the arena of javelin. For example, Jakub Vadlejch won the Diamond League in 2017, Magnus Kirt won in 2019 and Johannes Vetter won in 2021.

Reminiscing about his first event, Neeraj remembered how he had outdone some of the top athletes. He competed with all his heart. He was not the centre of attention, and that suited him perfectly as there was no pressure. Hence, the only focus was on giving his very best. Further, it helped to compete against such stalwarts. The exposure gave him the

---

[74]Paris Results, Diamond League, 2017, https://www.diamondleague.com/lists-results/archive/2017/. Accessed on 29 November 2021.

confidence such that it did not matter who was competing against him. His only focus was on being Neeraj Chopra!

Asian Athletics Championship, July 2017

A week later, Neeraj participated in the 22nd Asian Athletics Championship in Bhubaneshwar, Odisha. Athletes from all over Asia had converged at the Kalinga Stadium. Here Neeraj was the star. Now and then, the compere would remind spectators that they were in the presence of the 'world junior champion'. His face would flash on the giant screens whenever they announced his name.

His performance at Paris had only raised hopes of him winning the gold here. While his start was slow, Neeraj finished the event with his best effort of 85.23 m. He bettered his Paris mark and also won the gold!

'I was not feeling good initially, and it took time for me to hit my stride. I knew I just needed one big throw. I also felt that I was capable of doing it. But somehow, in the early part of the competition, I just did not feel the rush. But I knew that I just needed to switch on, and for me, it happened at the right time,' Neeraj said.[75] Another Indian thrower, Davinder Singh Kang won the bronze medal with a throw of 83.29 m.

---

[75] Koshie, Nihal. 'Asian Athletics Championship: Slumbering Neeraj Chopra Wakes Up in Time', *The Indian Express*, 10 July 2017, https://indianexpress.com/article/sports/sport-others/slumbering-neeraj-chopra-wakes-up-in-time-4743357/. Accessed on 29 November 2021.

Diamond League, Monaco, 21 July

Two weeks later, Neeraj was in Monaco participating in the Diamond League. Neeraj's performance had dropped now. His best was 78.92 m—considerably short of what he had been throwing recently.[76]

World Championship, August London

In the first half of August 2017, the city of London hosted the sixteenth edition of the IAAF World Championships in Athletics at the London stadium. Twenty-five competitors from India participated in 14 events. In the javelin throw, Davinder Singh Kang and Neeraj Chopra were representing India. Kang's 84.22 m and Neeraj's 82.26 m were not good enough to win India a medal. Worse, India failed to win any medal in the event. A country of over 1.3 billion did not have one athlete who could win even a bronze medal in world athletics. That was something!

Neeraj's performance also raised many questions. He had made throws over 83 m in the year already. He had been consistent; more so, his best came in third or the final throw. But this was a total departure from his recent performances.

Some argued there may have been pressure on him, while others questioned his technique. Deputy national

---

[76]Monaco Results, Diamond League, 2017, https://www.diamondleague.com/lists-results/archive/2017/. Accessed on 29 November 2021.

coach Radhakrishnan Nair pointed that Neeraj was travelling a lot and had missed training sessions after Bhubaneswar. He argued that Neeraj should have focused on training rather than competing in the Monaco Diamond League. There was also another reason that no one brought up—he had been competing without a coach. Calvert had left in May, and AFI had roped in Uwe Hohn of Germany, who would join only in September.[77]

A significant feat of the tournament was that Davinder Singh Kang became the first Indian to reach the final of the World Championship. However, Kang's fortunes took a nosedive when he found himself buried deep in doping controversies in 2018, which have hindered his career progress to date.

Diamond League, Zurich, 2017

The IAAS Diamond league final 2017 was held in Zurich on 23 and 24 August 2017. Neeraj was the only Indian to participate in the event. On the second day, he threw his best effort of 83.80 m during his first throw where he was also the first one to perform.

On his third throw, the javelin reached 83.39 m. He

---

[77]'Why Neeraj Chopra Failed to Qualify for IAAF World Championship Finals', *Hindustan Times*, 11 August 2017, https://www.hindustantimes.com/other-sports/iaaf-world-championships-neeraj-chopra-fails-to-qualify-for-javelin-throw-final/story-hxFBmseXkJ7xJsQ7vWSNoK.html. Accessed on 29 November 2021.

ended up seventh in the final list of eight.[78] Neeraj was 19 years old then. It was during his third throw that he injured his groin. Consequently, he stopped in his run-up in the fourth round and could not attempt in the fifth and sixth.

Jakub Vadlejch of Czech Republic (88.50 m) won the 2017 Diamond league, and German Thomas Rohler (86.59 m) came in second.[79]

Neeraj returned home pocketing a few thousand dollars from his Diamond League appearances but now it was time to recover. He had already had a jam-packed season. Lack of rest and recovery may have caused this injury. Consequently, Neeraj did not participate in any other event that year.[80]

In an interview, Neeraj said, 'I participated in about ten competitions. Before that, I probably did only three or four a year. I was not used to the travel and the training schedule between competitions. Most of them were competitions in which the best in the world participated so there was also pressure of expectations. I guess it all got a little too much. Because of the constant travel, I was not able to follow a proper diet, rest enough and also could not focus enough

---

[78]Zurich Results, Diamond League, 2017, https://www.diamondleague.com/lists-results/archive/2017/. Accessed on 29 November 2021.
[79]Ibid.
[80]PTI. 'Neeraj Chopra Suffers Groin Injury in Zurich Diamond League Finals', *The Indian Express*, 25 August 2017, https://indianexpress.com/article/sports/sport-others/neeraj-chopra-suffers-groin-injury-in-zurich-diamond-league-finals-4813150/. Accessed on 29 November 2021.

on training. I did not have time for recovery. This is one of the reasons why I got injured and was not able to throw to my potential.[81]

Offenburg, Germany

By this time, Uwe Hohn had arrived in India. He was a legend in the world of javelin throws, credited with breaking the 100-m mark more than three decades ago.

There was confusion in the Indian camp. With support from JSW, Neeraj was on rehabilitation. Werner Daniels was expecting him in Germany in early November. If Hohn was here now, who was he supposed to coach? This also created some turmoil in the federation. Ultimately, Kang began training with Hohn in Patiala. Alongside, Shivpal also started. Annu Rani, meanwhile, continued with Kashinath Naik.[82]

---

[81]Koshie, Nihal. 'Neeraj Chopra Reboots along the Rhine', *The Indian Express*, 22 February 2018, https://indianexpress.com/article/sports/sport-others/neeraj-chopra-reboots-along-the-rhine-5073383/. Accessed on 29 November 2021.

[82]Rayan, Stan. 'Hohn Is Here, Neeraj in a Dilemma', *The Hindu*, 26 October 2017, https://www.thehindu.com/sport/athletics/hohn-is-here-neeraj-in-a-dilemma/article19926941.ece. Accessed on 29 November 2021.

Werner Daniels

Having realized that his body could not take it, Neeraj decided to get off the competition treadmill, especially because 2017 was full of competitions. Since Calvert had left, he was also training on his own. That was nothing new for him, but now the stakes had risen considerably. He had now developed into a national hope. The sports federation and enthusiasts had started to look up to this young man with the hope that he could lift the spirits of Indian athletics.

The year 2018 was going to see the Commonwealth Games and the Asian Games. It was, therefore, important for Neeraj to utilize this off-season time to the very best. Time was of the essence. Neeraj had a short stint in Germany before the London World Championships but returned in November 2017.

Werner Daniels had previously trained 2013 Moscow Worlds Champion Christina Obergföll. Christina's husband, Boris, was then training world champion Johannes Vetter. Daniels was also close to Vetter. Realizing that it would be the best choice for him to train, learn and be inspired from Vetter, Neeraj packed his bags and left on a three-month visa to train in Germany.

Neeraj reached Offenburg in Germany, a border city with a population of less than 60,000, some 112 km from the River Rhine. Neeraj knew that it would be cold, but it was still colder than expected. However, most of his training was indoors. Still, there were days when he trained in the snow. The temperatures would fall to sub-zero levels, but that did not hinder him, for he was there for a purpose.

His training sessions included a variety of exercises, which were unknown to his Panipat group back in India. Neeraj focused on each body part, honing it to perfection. The focus was on building core strength and power. So, drills would include barbell press, barbell squats or the improvised version of Pilates.

Before meeting Daniels, he had spent a month rehabilitating at the IIS facility in Vijayanagar. He consciously decided to stay away from throwing for a while. His body was still recovering from the groin injury. Hence, the focus was to get the body in the best possible shape and increase core strength. Only in the last month did he start some throws. The idea was to stay injury-free for a long time.[83]

Those months in Germany were quite fruitful for Neeraj. He also had the opportunity to re-examine his technique. He added, 'My throwing hand was very low, and because of that my range was affected. Minor changes in technique can make a big difference in javelin throwing because it is a technical event. Small mistakes can set you back. Now, my hand stays higher. There are so many things you have to keep in mind, and having a coach around can really help.'[84]

---

[83]Koshie, Nihal. 'Neeraj Chopra Reboots along the Rhine', *The Indian Express*, 22 February 2018, https://indianexpress.com/article/sports/sport-others/neeraj-chopra-reboots-along-the-rhine-5073383/. Accessed on 29 November 2021.
[84]Ibid.

Those three months also helped Neeraj take his mind off the competition circuit. He lived in a rented apartment with his physiotherapist, cleaned the house and cooked food. Notably, Neeraj was a vegetarian. He had been living away from home for many years and had learnt how to cook. However, in 2016 there was a national camp in Poland. It was challenging to find vegetarian food there. Moreover, he was feeling a little weak. That is when he began eating chicken.[85]

Neeraj also travelled locally on his off days. Daniels took him to Strasbourg, right across the border in France. It was a 45-minute journey and a good break![86] By the end of the training, Neeraj started to make a few throws too. During his training, he also met Johannes Vetter. Vetter used to train in the same premises but their training timings were different.[87] Seeing the world champion training in the same facility would boost Neeraj's spirits. The two also competed in an event. Vetter came first and Neeraj second with 82.80 m.

In February, Neeraj returned to India and joined the national camp at Patiala. With increased core strength and a fresh mind, he was raring to go.

---

[85]Ibid.
[86]Ibid.
[87]PTI. 'Javelin Thrower Neeraj Chopra Aims for Medal and Personal Best at CWG', *News 18*, 4 March 2018, https://www.news18.com/news/other-sports/javelin-thrower-neeraj-chopra-aims-for-medal-and-personal-best-at-cwg-1678115.html. Accessed on 29 November 2021.

Federation Cup

Soon after Neeraj got back, the 22nd National Senior Federation cup began in Patiala, between 5 and 8 March. He had a slow start with a sub-80-m performance in the preliminaries. Even in the final, his best attempt only came in his last throw at 85.94 m. He still bettered the meet record that he had set the previous year. This was also around four metres better than the qualification mark for Commonwealth Games scheduled for later that year.

Notably, after returning to Patiala, Neeraj requested Hohn to continue with the plan Daniels had set for him. Neeraj had been training as per that plan, and tampering with it could have damaged his prospects. Hohn understood, and Neeraj kept returning for any suggestions from the national coach.

Commonwealth Games, 2018

Neeraj headed to the Gold Coast, in Queensland Australia, for the XXI Commonwealth Games the following month. A total of 216 athletes participated in 15 sporting events. Making its eighteenth appearance at the Games, India won 26 gold medals out of 66, finishing third in the tournament.

Neeraj entered the arena in a sky-blue vest and shorts. He had long hair and wore a bandana to keep them in control. With a thunderous run, he released his javelin to win the gold with his season's best throw of 86.47 m.

The qualifying rounds were held on 13 April and he made history the next day in the afternoon. Australian Hamish Peacock came second with an 82.59-m throw and Anderson Peters came third with 82.20 m. Another Indian, Vipin Kasana, came fifth in the event.[88]

Sotteville Athletics Meet

In July 2018, Neeraj continued his top performance by winning the gold at France's Meeting International de Sotteville-lès-Rouen. Neeraj, very impressively, did not falter in any attempt and completed all his rounds. His gold medal-winning throw of 85.17 m came in the fifth attempt, comfortably ahead of Moldova's silver medallist Andrian Mardare.[89]

Diamond League, 2018

It was clear that Neeraj considered the Diamond League a very important event in his competing schedule. The league brought together the very best and Neeraj took much joy in

---

[88]Result-Men's Javelin Throw Final, *Gold Coast*, https://results.gc2018.com/en/athletics/result-men-s-javelin-throw-fnl-000100-.htm. Accessed on 29 November 2021.

[89]'Neeraj Chopra Wins Gold at Sotteville Athletics Meet in France', Athletics Federation of India, 18 July 2018, https://indianathletics.in/neeraj-chopra-wins-gold-at-sotteville-athletics-meet-in-france/. Accessed on 29 November 2021.

putting his best foot forward. In 2018, Neeraj participated in Diamond League events in Doha, Eugene, Rabat and Zurich.

- Neeraj finished fourth, but more notably he made a new national record with his personal best at 87.43 m. (Doha, Qatar; 4 May 2018).[90]
- Eugene, Oregon, US; 27–28 May 2018; 80.81 m.[91]
- Rabat, Morocco; 13 July 2018; 83.32 m.[92]

Hence, during the final of the IAAF Diamond League in Zurich on 29 and 30 August, Neeraj finished fourth with a throw of 85.73 m.[93]

Finland

The Scandinavian countries have for the longest time been famous for javelin throws. A disproportionately high number of Olympic medallists in the javelin discipline have been from this region. Finland, especially, is considered the spiritual home of the javelin. There are a few reasons for it. For instance, it is believed that the javelin throw was an everyman sport in Finland. 'In the countryside, any small boy

---

[90]Doha Results, Diamond League, 2018, https://www.diamondleague.com/lists-results/archive/2018/. Accessed on 29 November 2021.

[91]Eugene Results, Diamond League, 2018, https://www.diamondleague.com/lists-results/archive/2018/. Accessed on 29 November 2021.

[92]Rabat Results, Diamond League, 2018, https://www.diamondleague.com/lists-results/archive/2018/. Accessed on 29 November 2021.

[93]Zurich Results, Diamond League, 2018, https://www.diamondleague.com/lists-results/archive/2018/. Accessed on 29 November 2021.

could make a rudimentary birch or alder javelin and throw it in any open field. Throwing things, along with lifting stones, putting shots, wrestling arms, climbing trees, etc., has always been part of Finnish physical exercise tradition.'[94] [95]

There is another opinion: Finns found a release of all their pent-up feelings when they threw the javelin. The extremities of the climate there have moulded Finnish psychology. Even more, it was a survival thing! The spear was a hunting weapon.

Regardless, for long, this region has been the hotbed for javelin throwers. Preceding the Asian Games, the 2018 national camp was organized in Finland by coach Hohn. A newspaper wrote, 'Chopra will be part of the national camp in Finland from 10 May to 22 June. The camp will be for throwers—shot-put, discuss and javelin—and the athletes will return to India to participate in the inter-state meet in Guwahati from 26 to 29 June, which will also act as qualifiers for the Asiad.'[96]

---

[94]Tomizawa, Roy. 'The Javelin Hotbed of Scandinavia', *The Olympians*, 27 May 2016, https://theolympians.co/2016/05/27/the-javelin-hotbed-of-scandinavia/. Accessed on 29 November 2021.

[95]Singh, Navneen. 'Seven Javelin Throwers to Train in Finland Ahead of 2018 Asian Games', *Hindustan Times*, 8 May 2018, https://www.hindustantimes.com/other-sports/six-javelin-throwers-to-train-in-finland-ahead-of-2018-asian-games/story-tkDOg0wPTlIiCzFd2I3OnI.html. Accessed on 29 November 2021.

[96]Hussain, Sabi. 'Neeraj Chopra to Train with Uwe Hohn in Finland', *The Times of India*, 2 May 2018, https://timesofindia.indiatimes.com/sports/more-sports/others/neeraj-chopra-to-train-with-uwe-hohn-in-finland/articleshow/63994507.cms. Accessed on 29 November 2021.

Incidentally, Neeraj was allowed to skip these qualifiers because he was already throwing well past the qualifying mark of 82 m. Another thrower, Shivpal Singh, qualified for the Asian Games with a throw of 82.28 m at the inter-state championships.

During the camp, Neeraj was allowed to participate in different competitions in Europe, which he began with the Diamond League in Doha on 4 May.

ം

Another thing one could not miss was Neeraj's performance vis-à-vis other players on the national circuit. In the 2018 Indian Grand Prix, on 27 February 2018, Neeraj threw 82.88 m and the silver medallist Vipin Kasana was at 80.04 m. The story was similar in the Federation Cup in March, where barring Neeraj (85.94 m) no other Indian could cross the 80-m mark.[97]

By this time, Hohn's training style were raising questions. However, it was hoped that the Finland tour would make a difference.[98]

---

[97] Indian Grand Prix Result, Athletic Federation of India, https://indianathletics.in/afi_result/indian-grand-prix-1-2/. Accessed on 29 November 2021.

[98] Singh, Navneet. 'Seven Javelin Throwers to Train in Finland ahead of 2018 Asian Games', *Hindustan Times*, 8 May 2018, https://www.hindustantimes.com/other-sports/six-javelin-throwers-to-train-in-finland-ahead-of-2018-asian-games/story-tkDOg0wPTlIiCzFd2I3OnI.html. Accessed on 29 November 2021.

~

Neeraj's top form continued at the Savo Games, at the end of July 2018. The event was in Lapinlahti, Finland, where he led with a throw of 85.69 m. His rival from Taipei, Chao-Tsun Cheng, came second with 82.52 m. Cheng was also the only Asian to have thrown beyond 90 m. But his performance had been inconsistent. And when it comes to mindset, Neeraj was at the top of his game from the beginning.[99]

Neeraj continued in Finland and spent three to four months training there. *The Indian Express* published a short piece written by him while he was still there. It sounded like a romantic longing for Finland. Here it is produced in full, dated 12 August 2018:

> Kuortane is such a scenic and peaceful place to train at. It was a little odd for me in the beginning as there are hardly any people here. I have heard that there are not even 10 people per square kilometre in this municipality of Finland. For an Indian this place almost seems deserted. The Olympic Centre where we train is also a little cut off from the rest of the region but it's a blessing in disguise.

---

[99]PTI. 'Neeraj Chopra Wins Javelin Gold at Savo Games', *ESPN*, 30 July 2018, https://www.espn.in/olympics/story/_/id/24230725/javelin-thrower-neeraj-chopra-wins-gold-savo-games-finland. Accessed on 29 November 2021.

We get to train peacefully and there are no disturbances. My focus is on training. The centre is located on the banks of the breath-taking Kuortane Lake. I didn't get much time to venture out and explore the area but a quiet walk along the lake shore is something I love doing. Even though this place is out of the world I still feel my hometown is a touch more serene than Kuortane.

Haryana has its own charms. I have visited home just once in the last year or so but now I have gotten used to staying away from home. I stay in touch through WhatsApp but I try to keep interactions minimal. All my time and energy is consumed by the sport. Even during my free time, I watch YouTube videos on javelin throwing. I also carry a Bluetooth speaker at all times and whenever I find time, I like to blast some Punjabi music in my room. Initially, it was difficult for me to get adjusted to the food but now it's fine. Though I don't even know what the dishes they serve here are called.

I find it the same throughout Europe— some chicken, salad, yogurt and lot of bread. To be honest, you get a lot of *ghaas phoos* (leafy salads) in Europe. I grew up as a strict vegetarian and one eats no non-vegetarian food at home. But when I started travelling abroad for competitions and training, I realized that the options are limited. So, I started eating chicken.

I know basic cooking and can make sabzi and nice

paranthas. But it's nowhere close to what you get in Haryana. The rotis baked on earthen stoves using upplas (cow-dung cakes) have a distinct taste that cannot be replicated. In Haryana they will feed you even if you're full.

Saying no is not an option. Paranthas back home are served with dollops of home-made butter, after being fried in ghee. And there's nothing like a big glass of lassi to wash it down. In Europe there is no dearth of variety but 'ghar ki roti mein jo baat hai, woh aur kahan, ji? [the taste of homemade food is unparalleled].'[100]

Good memories were made even as intense sessions were completed. Neeraj was ready for the Asian Games.

Asian Games, 2018

The 2018 Asian Games, officially known as the 18th Asian Games were also known as Jakarta-Palembang 2018. The Asian Games are a multi-sport event where athletes from all countries of Asia converge to the host city to compete. As many as 45 nations sent their official delegations. The Games were in two cities of Indonesia—the capital Jakarta, and Palembang in the southern Sumatra region. They were held from 18 August to 2 September 2021.

---

[100] 'Neeraj Chopra: Finding Peace in Finnish Backyard', *The Indian Express*, 12 August 2018, https://indianexpress.com/article/sports/asian-games/neeraj-chopra-finding-peace-in-finnish-backyard-5302523/. Accessed on 29 November 2021.

During the send-off ceremony organized for the Indian contingent, IOA President Narinder Batra announced that Neeraj would be the flagbearer at the opening ceremony. Neeraj, then training in Finland, told PTI, 'I am thrilled to be chosen as flag bearer of the Asian Games. It is a huge honour to be leading the Indian contingent at such a big event. I did not know this as I was not told earlier. This is going to be my first (to be a flag bearer) and it's happening in the Asian Games.'[101] Consequently, Neeraj reached Jakarta much earlier than the day of his event.

The opening ceremony was on 18 August. Olympic medallist Sushil Kumar said while speaking to ANI, 'He (Neeraj Chopra) is our future Olympic champion. Chopra has got the calibre to win an Olympic medal, which this country is dreaming of, for a long time.'[102]

The Games witnessed Neeraj breaking his national record of 87.43 m which he had created a few months earlier at the Doha Diamond League event. Neeraj was confident right from the beginning. He began with 83.46 m and his second throw was rejected. It was the third throw which went far up to 88.06 m. He won the gold but missed

---

[101]PTI. 'Neeraj Named Flag-Bearer for Asian Games Opening Ceremony', *The Hindu*, 10 August 2018, https://www.thehindu.com/sport/athletics/neeraj-named-flag-bearer-for-asian-games-opening-ceremony/article24655507.ece. Accessed on 29 November 2021.

[102]Neeraj Chopra Is the Future Olympian: Sushil Kumar', *Asia News International*, 18 August 2018, https://www.google.com/search?q=ani+full+form+in+news&oq=ANI+full+&aqs=chrome.2.69i57j0i433i512j0i512l8.3956j0j7&sourceid=chrome&ie=UTF-8. Accessed on 29 November 2021.

the meet record by around one metre.

Nevertheless, Neeraj had won India's second gold in athletics and eighth overall. Neeraj said, 'The competition was good, I had trained well and was focused on getting a gold medal for the country.' He stood there on the podium shining and smiling, wearing a dark blue jacket, with the Indian National Flag around his shoulders, holding the Games mascot. He was the Asian Games Gold medallist and India's Olympic hope from Khandra.[103]

Shivpal Singh had to pull out midway from the event due to a shoulder injury. The nation last finished on the podium in the javelin discipline back at the 1982 Asian Games in New Delhi, when Gurtej Singh won a bronze for the nation.[104]

The medal ceremony also got famous for another thing. The final standings put Neeraj with the gold at 88.06 m. Chinese Liu Qizhen was second at 82.22 m and Arshad Nadeem from Pakistan won the bronze with a throw of 80.75 m. As the winners stood on the podium after the medals presentation, India's national anthem reverberated through the stadium complex. This was what the athletes

---

[103]'Asian Games 2018: Neeraj Chopra Wins First India's First Gold In Javelin Throw, Sets New National Record', *The Indian Express*, 28 August 2018, https://indianexpress.com/article/sports/asian-games/asian-games-2018-neeraj-chopra-becomes-first-indian-javelin-thrower-to-win-gold-at-asiads-sets-new-national-record-5327563/. Accessed on 29 November 2021.
[104]Ibid.

competed for. These were the moments all the effort was for!

A picture with Neeraj congratulating Arshad Nadeem also made news all over. It was a gesture of sportsmanship and respect for what the young men had achieved. People on social media, however, took liberty with their comments!'

The champion flew out of Jakarta quickly to take part in the Diamond League final in Zurich, just hours after winning the gold![105]

～

The Diamond League final pitted Neeraj against the eight best javelin throwers in the world. 2017's Diamond League winner Jakub Vadlejch of the Czech Republic threw a season-best of 89.02 m. Rio Olympic winner Thomas Roehler and Andreas Hofmann had thrown above the 90-m mark during the season. Neeraj was in the premier league. He was getting the best out of his game and learning in the process.

According to a report, going by the season's best, Chopra was fifth among the eight competitors, but he had qualified as sixth-best in terms of points. Participating in three Diamond League Series legs, he had a total of 12

---

[105] PTI. 'Asian Games 2018: Neeraj Chopra Leaves for Diamond League Final Hours after Winning Historic Gold', *Firstpost*, 28 August 2018, https://www.firstpost.com/sports/asian-games-2018-neeraj-chopra-leaves-for-diamond-league-final-hours-after-winning-historic-gold-5063611.html. Accessed on 29 November 2021.

points. He finished fourth in Doha, sixth in Eugene and fifth in Rabat. He could not participate in the Birmingham leg on 18 August due to the Asian Games.[106]

At Zurich now, Neeraj was a medal hopeful till the fifth round with a best throw of 85.73 m until Thomas Roehler threw a marginally better one of 85.76 m in his last attempt. Neeraj missed a bronze by just 0.03 m.[107]

It was a loss but Neeraj believed his best tournament in 2018 was the Diamond League. You have to understand that in the CWG and the Asiad, only a select group of countries participated. It is in the Diamond League that the best athletes on the planet converged. For an athlete targeting top glory in his field of play, a win in the Diamond League was the ultimate prize.[108]

IAAF Continental Cup

Following the 30 August Diamond League performance, Neeraj headed for the Continental Cup. The AAA selected seven top athletes to represent an Asia-Pacific Team in the International Association of Athletics Federation

---

[106]Ibid.

[107]Zurich Results, Diamond League, 2018, https://www.diamondleague.com/lists-results/archive/2018/. Accessed on 29 November 2021.

[108]PTI. 'Asian Games 2018 Gold Medallist Neeraj Chopra Misses Bronze by a Whisker at Diamond League Final in Zurich', *Firstpost*, 31 August 2018, https://www.firstpost.com/sports/asian-games-2018-gold-medallist-neeraj-chopra-misses-bronze-by-a-whisker-at-diamond-league-final-in-zurich-5086251.html. Accessed on 29 November 2021.

(IAAF) Continental Cup to be held in Ostrava, the Czech Republic.[109] Ostrava is the third largest city of the Czech Republic and Neeraj was then training in Finland with Hohn.

Neeraj entered the competition as the best hope for India. Johannes Vetter and Andreas Hofmann were not taking part. Thomas Roehler was everyone's favourite having bagged the European title.[110]

The IAAF rules allowed three throws to each athlete. Only one player advanced to the finals from each team. Neeraj threw 80.24 m followed by 79.76 m. His third attempt was rather good on distance crossing the 85-m mark but it fell out of the sector by just a few centimetres. Neeraj was disqualified, and at his expense, his Asia-Pacific teammate Chao-Tsun Cheng progressed to the semi-finals. Thomas Roehler clinched the gold.

But what broke the hearts of his family back in India was how disappointed Neeraj was. Uncle Bhim could see it through while watching the Games. As soon as Neeraj's javelin left his hand, he knew he had thrown a good one.

---

[109]'Akhil Nair, Neeraj Chopra, Hima Das to Represent Asia-Pacific in Continental Cup', *News 18*, 28 July 2018, https://www.news18.com/news/sports/neeraj-chopra-hima-das-to-represent-asia-pacific-in-continental-cup-1826747.html. Accessed on 29 November 2021.

[110]Sen, Turja. 'IAAF Continental Cup 2018: Focus on Neeraj Chopra as India's Asian Games Stars Look to Shine in Ostrava Event', *Firstpost*, 7 September 2018, https://www.firstpost.com/sports/iaaf-continental-cup-2018-focus-on-neeraj-chopra-as-indias-asian-games-stars-look-to-shine-in-ostrava-event-5135561.html. Accessed on 29 November 2021.

But he kept looking at it till it landed. He knew its course had shifted to the left. As the javelin landed, he slapped the run-up track in utter frustration. It was a good effort but counted as no-throw.

However, as he composed himself, it is remarkable to note what he felt. Speaking to *India Today*, Neeraj said, 'It was really disappointing to lose out on a medal by a whisker. I had a throw beyond 85 m, but it went out of the sector. It is something I need to work on during the off-season. This is not the first time that my javelin landed close to the boundary of the sector, and it only showed that I need to improve my technique.'[111]

He knew he did not need to make significant changes in his technique, but he needed to control the left tilts. Owing to a very tight schedule, he had been unable to spend time on improving his throws. But he realized that he had to reduce the flight in his throw and keep it as straight as possible with the same strength. His old habits from Panchkula continued.

∽

Notably, Triple jumper Arpinder Singh created history by becoming the first Indian to win a medal in the IAAF

---

[111]Halder, Aditya K. 'Neeraj Chopra Seeks Improvement', *India Today*, 12 September 2018, https://www.indiatoday.in/mail-today/story/neeraj-chopra-seeks-improvement-1338343-2018-09-12. Accessed on 29 November 2021.

Continental Cup when he clinched a bronze with an effort of 16.59 m.[112]

Arjuna Award, 2018

In September 2018, for all his achievements in the field of athletics, Naib Subedar Neeraj Chopra was conferred with the Arjuna Award. Wearing the customized maroon blazer and grey pants, Neeraj received the award at the Rashtrapati Bhawan from the honourable President Shri Ramnath Kovind.[113] In November of the same year, Neeraj was given an out-of-turn promotion for his spectacular performance in 2018. From Naib Subedar, Neeraj became a Subedar in the Indian Army.[114]

---

[112]PTI. 'IAAF Continental Cup 2018: Arpinder Singh Clinches Bronze Medal in Triple Jump, Neeraj Chopra Finishes Sixth', *Firstpost*, 9 September 2018, https://www.firstpost.com/sports/iaaf-continental-cup-2018-arpinder-singh-clinches-bronze-medal-in-triple-jump-neeraj-chopra-finishes-sixth-5149191.html. Accessed on 29 November 2021.

[113]Das, Saptarshi. 'Throwback to Time When Neeraj Chopra Won Arjuna Award in 2018 after Commonwealth Games', *RepublicWorld.com*, 7 August 2021, https://www.republicworld.com/sports-news/other-sports/throwback-to-time-when-neeraj-chopra-won-arjuna-award-in-2018-after-commonwealth-games.html. Accessed on 29 November 2021.

[114]Philip, Snehesh Alex. 'With Olympics "Golden Throw", Subedar Neeraj Chopra Could Land Promotion in Army', *The Print*, 8 August 2021, https://theprint.in/india/with-olympics-golden-throw-subedar-neeraj-chopra-could-land-promotion-in-army/711237/. Accessed on 29 November 2021.

Camp South Africa, 2019

In January 2019, four male throwers—Rajinder Singh, Shivpal Singh, Sahil Silwal and Neeraj, with coach Uwe Hohn reached a high-altitude centre at North-West University in Potchefstroom, South Africa. Hohn had been consistently complaining about the lack of facilities and shortage of staff at Patiala. In contrast, at North-West University, training equipment, food and nutrition, medical support and physiotherapy was 'very good'.[115]

The delay in the camp and cancellation of another camp in Australia had disappointed Hohn, who thought the team was behind schedule. More so for Neeraj, Hohn had things planned, but it was Neeraj's elbow which was causing excruciating pain. According to the coach this was because of the low-arm technique Neeraj had self-learnt or through videos. And it was his throwing arm!

Many javelin throwers complain of or even undergo procedures related to the elbow or shoulders because this is where maximum force and movement happens when the athlete releases the javelin.

---

[115]Koshie, Nihal. 'Neeraj Chopra Is Six Weeks behind Schedule, Says Coach Uwe Hohn', *The Indian Express*, 14 February 2019, https://indianexpress.com/article/sports/sport-others/javelin-thrower-neeraj-chopra-is-six-weeks-behind-schedule-5582782/. Accessed on 29 November 2021.

Injury and Hiatus

> *'Time teaches something every time and I have learnt a lot in this period both on and off the field. All of it will help me in the future.'*
>
> —Neeraj Chopra to *Sportstar* in September at NIS Patiala. (Around four months after surgery)

However, Neeraj was in slight discomfort over the past few months. He was experiencing some sort of 'tightness in the shoulder and weakness in the back.'[116] Hence, he started drawing more strength from his elbow. Doctors conducted numerous scans and probes, but to no avail.

Neeraj was also being helped to overcome the elbow injury which had been affecting his throws since the middle of November 2018 by Potchefstroom-based physiotherapist, Anita van der Lingen.[117]

The 2019 season was about to begin, but Neeraj could not throw a single one without pain. At this point, Neeraj

---

[116] Hussain, Sabi. 'Was Javelin-Thrower Neeraj Chopra's Injury Mismanaged? *The Times of India*, 17 May 2019, https://timesofindia.indiatimes.com/sports/more-sports/athletics/was-javelin-thrower-neeraj-chopras-injury-mismanaged/articleshow/69368645.cms. Accessed on 29 November 2021.

[117] Koshie, Nihal. 'Neeraj Chopra Is Six Weeks behind Schedule, Says Coach Uwe Hohn', *The Indian Express*, 14 February 2019, https://indianexpress.com/article/sports/sport-others/javelin-thrower-neeraj-chopra-is-six-weeks-behind-schedule-5582782/. Accessed on 29 November 2021.

was sent to the Sir H.N. Reliance Foundation Hospital in Mumbai. Orthopaedic surgeon Dr Dinshaw Pardiwala and sports physiotherapist Heath Matthews, who worked as the head of sports medicine at the hospital, observed him.

According to an AFI source speaking to *The Times of India*, 'The physio wasn't able to find out this problem. If he was with Neeraj for 24 hours and was treating him, then he should have known that his shoulder wasn't good or that his shoulder wasn't reaching the range, therefore pushing and stressing the elbow. The minute we took him to the hospital, Dr Pardiwala and Heath said, "Hold on, this couldn't have happened to him and there's something else which is causing this. Let's go to the cause."'[118]

Following simple tests, specialists realized that Neeraj's shoulder was not opening, and the whole jerk was coming on the elbow rather than drawing from both shoulder and elbow. Further, Neeraj's lower back was weak, which meant he used his back sparingly for drawing strength. Hence the three parts to focus on were the lower back, shoulder and elbow.

Dhananjay Kaushik, head of sports science and physiotherapy at IIS, was also carefully observing Neeraj. In an interview, he said, 'We found loose bodies in the joint and eventually decided that he must undergo surgery

---

[118]Hussain, Sabi. 'Was Javelin-Thrower Neeraj Chopra's Injury Mismanaged? *The Times of India*, 17 May 2019, https://timesofindia.indiatimes.com/sports/more-sports/athletics/was-javelin-thrower-neeraj-chopras-injury-mismanaged/articleshow/69368645.cms. Accessed on 29 November 2021.

to remove them in May (2019). He could not get his elbow into full extension. The pain was terrible.'[119]

On 2 May, Neeraj underwent arthroscopic surgery on his elbow. Neeraj put a picture of him resting at the hospital with the sling around his shoulder to support the arm online. And thus began the rehabilitation process!

∽

Two weeks after the surgery, Neeraj was back at his workouts. He was at the IIS facility during this rehabilitation time. He would do two-hour workouts in the morning and 90-minute sessions in the evening. Mornings were primarily invested in full-body conditioning using medicine balls, bikes and core strengthening work. Evening sessions included motion exercises respecting the limitations of the elbow, which was still recovering.[120] His routine was closely maintained and regular training helped him a lot.[121]

A team of physiotherapists and sports scientists began

---

[119]Dhar, Pulasta. 'How Neeraj Chopra beat a serious injury on his road to gold', *Mint Lounge*, https://lifestyle.livemint.com/health/fitness/how-neeraj-chopra-beat-a-serious-injury-on-his-road-to-gold-111628685357804.html. Accessed on 8 December 2021.

[120]Dhar, Pulasta. 'How Neeraj Chopra Beat a Serious Injury on His Road to Gold', *Mint Lounge*, 12 August 2021, https://lifestyle.livemint.com/health/fitness/how-neeraj-chopra-beat-a-serious-injury-on-his-road-to-gold-111628685357804.html. Accessed on 29 November 2021.

[121]Ganesan, Uthra. 'Neeraj Chopra: It Was Not Easy Staying Patient During Rehab', *Sportstar*, 5 September 2019, https://sportstar.thehindu.com/athletics/neeraj-chopra-interview-javelin-injury-rehab-career-worlds/article29343461.ece. Accessed on 29 November 2021.

working on his wrist and improving other joints and muscles. Gradually, the focus shifted to the elbow. A hundred days post-surgery, Neeraj began throwing medicine balls of different weights. This was supposed to increase his core strength. He then shifted to stick and later to javelin. The best part was that Neeraj could now focus upon those small areas that had been neglected so far.

A little tweaking could make an impact on his performance. Where Neeraj stood, the idea was to add a few more centimetres, adding up to more metres.[122] He was now amongst the best in the world. There would be improvements by adding centimetres and inches and it would happen through minor tweaking which would help elevate his performance.

By September 2019, Neeraj was ready to throw a full-size javelin. His physiotherapist Ishan Marwaha, who stayed with him, remembered that day vividly. It was a tense situation and the team was nervous. The idea was to evaluate his body. The distance for the first time was not important.[123] Of course, it meant something else altogether for Neeraj. He said in an interview, 'I was training all this while but that moment of standing on the runway, the feeling of being a thrower, even when you are not doing

---

[122]Dhar, Pulasta. 'How Neeraj Chopra Beat a Serious Injury on His Road to Gold', *Mint Lounge*, 12 August 2021, https://lifestyle.livemint.com/health/fitness/how-neeraj-chopra-beat-a-serious-injury-on-his-road-to-gold-111628685357804.html. Accessed on 29 November 2021
[123]Ibid.

anything, is something that can only be felt by an athlete.'[124]

But, four months of no javelin! The body took its time to heal. It was not easy to stay patient, but there was no other choice. He had to remain positive. He remembers reading books and going to malls in Mumbai during the rehabilitation phase just to keep his mind straight.[125]

This surgery, however, meant that Neeraj missed most of the action in 2019. He missed the World Championships, Diamond Leagues and the Asian Championships. Still, four months later, he was back in Patiala at the national camp with Uwe Hohn.

∞

Neeraj's absence provided Shivpal with the opportunity to shine. Earlier, Shivpal had also suffered an elbow injury. At the Asian Games, he registered a throw of just 74.11 m.[126] The reason was a hairline fracture. Making a comeback now, he recorded a personal best of 86.23 m winning India a silver medal at the 2019 Asian Athletics Championships.

∞

---

[124]Ganesan, Uthra. 'Neeraj Chopra: It Was Not Easy Staying Patient During Rehab', *Sportstar*, 5 September 2019, https://sportstar.thehindu.com/athletics/neeraj-chopra-interview-javelin-injury-rehab-career-worlds/article29343461.ece. Accessed on 29 November 2021.
[125]Ibid.
[126]Koshie, Nihal. 'As Neeraj Chopra Recuperates from Injury, Shivpal Singh Emerges as India's Best Bet in Javelin', *The Indian Express*, 15 May 2019, https://indianexpress.com/article/sports/sport-others/as-neeraj-chopra-recuperates-from-an-injury-shivpal-singh-emerges-as-indias-best-bet-in-javelin-5727864/. Accessed on 29 November 2021.

In November, Neeraj parted ways with Uwe Hohn and joined bio-mechanics expert Klaus Bartonietz in South Africa. Bartonietz was hired in May to coach the growing pool of national campers and ease the burden on Hohn. During the rehabilitation phase, he had spent considerable time with Bartonietz, which helped the transition. The decision taken by the AFI was to facilitate Neeraj as he prepared for the Tokyo Olympics 2020.

Said an AFI official, 'Keeping the preference of the athlete in mind, we decided to allow him to train with Bartonietz. Chopra respected Hohn because it was while training with him that he won the Asian Games and the Commonwealth Games gold and set the national record. However, he wanted a change when it came to the training method. Chopra believed that he might not be able to handle the volume of workload Hohn would have wanted him to. He has trained with Hohn for two years, and there was nothing wrong in wanting to train with Bartonietz. There is nothing personal about wanting to change the coach.'[127]

Neeraj was also advised against attending any event. After all, the AFI and SAI knew that the entire nation was hoping for an athletics medal from him at the Tokyo Olympics. The first one!

---

[127]Koshie, Nihal. 'Neeraj Chopra No Longer Training with High-Profile Coach Hohn', *The Indian Express*, 30 November 2019, https://indianexpress.com/article/sports/neeraj-chopra-no-longer-training-with-high-profile-coach-uwe-hohn-6143382/. Accessed on 29 November 2021.

8

Man with the Golden Arm

India at the Olympics

Writer Boria Mazumdar and Nalin Mehta wrote 'As John MacAloon argues, the Olympics are a "crucible of symbolic force" into which the world pours its energies and a stage upon which, every four years, it plays "out its hopes and its terrors". For every Indian, that terror always came in the form of a question: a billion people and no gold medal.'[128]

---

[128] Boria Majumdar and Nalin Mehta. *Olympics—The India Story*, HarperCollins, 2012, p. 8.

1900–1948

We can narrate the history of India at the Olympics from many angles. From Major Dhyan Chand, the legendary Hockey player collecting three gold medals in three Olympics [1928, 1932 and 1936], to the glass-shattering exploits of Karnam Malleswari's weightlifting bronze at the 2000 Sydney Olympics. There could be another narrative—the rise of Indian athletes after 1947.

Whichever narrative one chooses, the story's arc is the same—athletes overachieving in the eyes of the world—the unlikeliest of heroes. This is against a backdrop of little or no facilities, lack of world class coaching or, in some cases, not even possessing the funds to attend the Games.

India's journey to the Olympics has two beginnings. The first would be the 1900 Olympics. Then still under Britain's occupation, with a loanee athlete named Norman Pritchard, born in Calcutta, sent to compete in the 200 m hurdles and 200 m sprint of the Paris Games. However, despite being born in India, he was regarded as competing for Britain. Interestingly, Pritchard later migrated to the US and became a silent movie actor.

In 1920, thanks to the efforts of Sir Dorabji Tata, the eldest son of Nusserwanji Tata, the founder of the Tata conglomerate, the International Olympic Committee recognized India as British Territory. In Sir Dorabji's words: 'Having been educated in my youth in England, I had shared in nearly every kind of English athletics and acquired a great love for them. On my return to India, I conceived the idea of introducing a love for such things there. I helped set up with the support of English friends, as general secretary, a High School Athletic Association amongst numerous schools of Bombay, in the first place for cricket, and then for athletics, sports meetings which embraced nearly all the events which form part of the Inter-University contests every year in London.'[129]

This led to the formation of the Deccan Gymkhana Club with Tata as its president. Impressed by what he was developing, he decided to send athletes at his own expense. Sadly, India did not win any medals at the first showing but it lit the spark for Indian athletes to follow.

'Subsequently, in 1923–24, a provisional All India Olympic Committee was set up, which organized the All India Olympic Games (that later became the National Games of India) in February 1924. Eight athletes from the Games were selected to represent India at the 1924 Paris Olympics. This provided the necessary impetus to the development and institutionalization of sports, which fructified with the formation of the Indian Olympic Association (IOA) in 1927. The IOA was formed, with Sir Dorabji Tata as its founding president and Dr A.G. Noehren as secretary.'[130]

---

[129]Ibid.

[130]Indian Olympic Association, https://olympic.ind.in/history. Accessed on 29 November 2021.

The 1924 Olympics was similar, showing a delegation of seven tennis players. However, things began to shift gears in 1927. With the time to prepare, scout talent and better organization, the 1928 Olympic Games was a watershed moment. Along with seven athletes, the British Indian delegation was joined by a strong hockey team which routed home nation, Netherlands, 3-0 in the finals. Charismatic and enigmatic Dhyan Chand score two goals and had a tally of 14 goals in the Games. The star of Indian hockey, Dhyan Chand was then a sepoy in the Army and a man who was not born into privileges.

Similar performances in the Colonial Era for the British Indian Olympic team followed at the 1932 and 1936 Games. The one in 1936 provided an incredible backdrop against the rise of Adolf Hitler's Nazi government and his 'master race' ideology. The incredible feats of Jesse Owens stole the headlines. However, on the hockey field, Major Dhyan Chand's India team launched a blitzkrieg of its own in the final destroying the German team 8–1 to win their third consecutive gold.

A rumour in the sports arena has it that Hitler personally met Dhyan Chand and offered him an officer's commission in the Wehrmacht if he would play for Germany. The story, however, is unverified because no contemporary source mentions it. Even Dhyan Chand made no mention of such a thing in his autobiography.

The Olympics in 1936 would be the final one under British rule as the next few Olympic Games would be interrupted first by World War I and then by India's partition in 1947. The IOA, now unrestrained by British policies and mismanagement, began sending bigger teams with better support staff. With the establishment of state teams and local clubs, the talent pool grew. At the 1948 Olympics, the first one under the Indian tricolour, the Indian hockey team met their old masters, Great Britain. Led by Captain Kishan Lal, India secured a 4–0 victory and won another gold.

1952–2021

In 1950, India qualified for the FIFA World Cup in Brazil because several other teams withdrew from the competition. However, the Indian team would not travel for a few reasons. Firstly, FIFA rejected their wish to play barefoot, and secondly, India rated the Olympics above the Football World Cup. Today that might be considered a short-sighted decision, but it speaks of the regard the Olympics held in the Indian consciousness at that time.

The successes of the hockey team and a resurgence of indigenous and traditional sports such as shooting and wrestling, coupled with a better organization at the local and regional levels, meant that pathways towards Olympic camps and trials were beginning to form. It is well encapsulated in Khashaba Dadasaheb Jadhav's journey to the medal and history books.

The 5'6" wrestler, popularly called 'Pocket Dynamo', from the village of Golleshwar in Karad, Satara, was born into a family with a wrestling heritage. He was surrounded by wrestlers since childhood and began training at the age of just five. Winning local and regional competitions put him on track for the Olympics. British coach Rees Gardner zeroed in on him after being impressed with his footwork and agility.

At this stage, one should note that the IOC always scrambled to find funding, usually from wealthier sections of Indian society and international contributions. Jadhav's story is the same: the Maharaja of Kolhapur, Shahji II, sponsored his first trip to the Olympics in 1948. The story remains unchanged today. However, the advent of TV and social media has allowed businesses to contribute through sponsorships.

∽

Kashaba Jadhav's first outing was not a success as he failed to win a medal. But the experience would prove to be invaluable. He was led by an experienced coach in a Western form of wrestling and trained diligently at a higher weight category of 125 lbs (56.7 kg). At the 1952 Olympics in Helsinki, he won a bronze for India, the country's first-ever individual medal. Jadhav's record-breaking achievement, whilst acknowledged in his village, did not garner much attention elsewhere.

Moreover, hockey glory overshadowed Jadhav's journey. His struggle to reach the Olympics was not an easy one. Back then, those representing the country in most sports had to fend for themselves and arrange their funding. Friends and neighbours helped out, with the shopkeepers of Karad arranging to buy his kit. The remarkable sacrifice of Khardekar, the principal of Raja Ram College, who sold his house to get the funds needed for the trip finally saw Jadhav on his way to Helsinki.

And if it were not for the 1948 Olympics financed by the Maharaja of Kolhapur, Shahaji II, Jadhav's route to an Olympic medal would have been a non-starter. Thanks to the trip, he trained rigorously under Reese Garder, the US lightweight champion, for a week before the Games.

Jadhav won the bronze and became a national icon. But was he treated like one? After Olympics glory, Jadhav's story is a case study on how India treated its best wrestler in the day. Maybe our priorities then were different. But remember this: Jadhav had to wait until 2001 to posthumously receive the Arjuna award for his lifelong contribution to Indian sports. Not only that, he sold his wife's jewels to build a modest cottage and ultimately died in poverty.[131]

---

[131]Boria Majumdar and Nalin Mehta. *Olympics—The India Story*, HarperCollins, 2012, p. 11.

A common theme with Indian athletes is the lack of a post-career support structure that has created a trend of tragic endings. Jadhav would become a police officer, but due to entanglements with his pension, he lived his later life in poverty, dying tragically in a road accident in 1984.

India has primarily remained an impoverished country; the morality of diverting funds from programmes that may feed people or medical programmes that save lives to fund athletes is a difficult one. Those with means largely formed the talent pool with mainstays such as hockey in which India dominated, convincingly winning gold at eight Olympics [1928, 1932, 1936, 1948, 1952, 1956, 1964 and 1980].

A sport that is achieving naturally attracts money and talent. The dominance of cricket in India is the best example of this, where success in the sport is a means for social mobility. The Olympics only happen every four years, not to mention the time taken to win local, regional and other international competitions. In the most likely event, an athlete's journey can hope for one or maybe two Olympics before succumbing to age, form or injury.

∽

Then there is the story of 'Flying Sikh' Milkha Singh whose position as the finest athlete produced by India is no longer uncontested. Champion sprinter Milkha won gold at both Asian and Commonweath Games. Displaced during partition, Milkha became an inspiration for Indian athletes for decades and his 1960 Rome Olympics sojourn is a tale for all ears.

It was his second Olympics, and he had come into the stage following a splendid show at the 1958 Asian Games where he had won a gold in 400 m in Tokyo. *The Hindu* described his training in some detail: 'India's great hope has been devoting between an hour and an hour and a half to training every day since his arrival in Rome. He is cutting the distances to sprints of about 150 yards with the object of speeding up. If he has not the stamina now, he will never have it.'[132]

Singh finished fourth despite having broken the Olympic record in a time of 45.6 seconds with a rare race where the first four finishers broke the existing world record.

The loss always rankled Milkha and he described it as the worst and best moment of his life. In his autobiography, he wrote: 'I started off by being ahead of the others, and at the 250-m mark, I was running so perilously fast that I decided to slow down in case I collapsed—a fatal decision I regret even to this day. As I completed 300 m, the three competitors right behind me came abreast and began to move ahead, and even though I increased my speed, trying desperately to catch up with Spence, who I had beaten at Cardiff, or the two before him, I could not wipe out the deficit of those six or seven yards. And thus, as fate would have it, my error of judgment at that crucial point in the

---

[132]Ibid. p. 279.

race, had dragged me to the fourth position and destroyed all my chances of winning that elusive Olympic gold.

Yet, it was a very close race, where the top positions were decided through a photo finish, which meant that the announcements were delayed. The suspense was excruciating. When the results were declared, all four of us—Davis, Kaufmann, Spence and I—had shattered the previous Olympic record of 45.9 seconds. Davis had come first with 44.9 seconds; Kaufmann was second with the same time of 44.9 seconds and Spence third with 45.5 seconds. Even though I had come fourth, my timing of 45.6 seconds was still a new record. I felt completely bereft and humiliated by what had happened.'[133]

Said Mazumdar and Mehta, 'Oh, Milkha! The first national heartbreak.'[134] Before Olympics and after it, Milkha remained the top star of Indian athletics. It was he who inspired generations after him.

∽

India's success at the Olympics was sporadic despite the Indian hockey team's dominance. That dominance is by no means small. If one looks at the medal tally over the years, apart from K.D. Jadhav's 1952 bronze; there are flashes of one medal each time. From 1928 to 1972! Then in 1976,

---

[133]Singh, Milkha. *The Race of My Life: An Autobiography*, Rupa Publications, 2013, p. 57.
[134]Majumdar, Boria and Mehta, Nalin. *Olympics—The India Story*, HarperCollins, 2012, p. 279.

we did not win that either, only to strike back in 1980 with another gold. From there till 1996, the Indian team came back empty-handed from each Olympics.

༄

And then, after decades, tennis legend Leander Paes won another individual medal. One can only imagine what that would have meant. It was 3 August 1996 when Paes defeated Brazilian Fernando Meligeni to win the bronze at the Atlanta Olympics. He has remained the star of Indian tennis, ever since. There can be no question that the economic reforms in 1991 and economic growth has meant more medals in recent times. Spurred on by the success of Indian Cricket, Indian businesses and a rise in living standards has been vital.

There is a direct correlation between money and medals. Arguably the most recent example of this is the UK. For each medal won by the UK at the Rio Olympics in 2016, there was an average spending of £5 million ($6.6 million). India only picked up two medals in those Games. The UK spends approximately $1.5 billion, which is ₹9,000 crore. This spending covers sports infrastructure and training. In comparison, UK sports bodies spent about $350 million on Olympics preparation between 2013–2017.

The rise in spending on Indian athletes and sports will undoubtedly mean more medals. The signs are already there. At the 2000 Olympics, weightlifter Karnam Malleswari became the first Indian woman to win an Olympic medal—a bronze in the 69 kg. Rajyvardhan Singh Rathore won silver in shooting in 2004. In 2008, Abhinav Bindra struck gold in shooting and Vijender Singh and Sushil Kumar won a bronze in boxing and freestyle wrestling.

However, the London 2012 Olympics saw the fruition of many years of planning and preparation. India sent a record delegation of 83 athletes and collected six medals in wrestling, badminton, boxing and shooting. The rise of social media and satellite television has allowed a nation to get swept up in the pomp and ceremony of the Olympics. Shooters Vijay Kumar and Gagan Narang, wrestlers Sushil Kumar and Yogeshwar Dutt, shuttler Saina Nehwal and boxer Mary Kom, all brought glory home and achieved instant stardom. Not resting on their laurels, the 2016 and 2021 Olympics saw again a record number of athletes—118 and 124, respectively—being sent.

Neeraj Targets 2020

'They say a lion always takes a step back before attacking, I think of a setback [injury] in an athlete's life is like that,' said Neeraj Chopra in March 2020.[135]

---

[135]Rebello, Maleeva. 'Olympics or Not, Javelin Star Neeraj Chopra Is Ready to Conquer', *The Economic Times*, 18 March 2020, https://economictimes.indiatimes.com/magazines/panache/olympics-or-not-javelin-star-neeraj-chopra-is-ready-to-conquer/articleshow/74683542.cms?from=mdr. Accessed on 29 November 2021.

In early 2020, competitions were held in South Africa where Neeraj and Shivpal qualified for the Tokyo Olympics. However, the Olympics, the peak event of the year, remained shrouded in uncertainty due to the COVID-19 pandemic. Not many realized the extent of the pandemic at that time. And as it happened, it saw the suspension of the entire 2021 domestic and international season.

Neeraj had missed the entire 2019 season too. He had tried to appear for the National Championship late in 2019. However, the AFI disagreed. Consequently, Neeraj had more time to heal and improve his core strength.

Since the last week of November 2019, Neeraj was in South Africa. He explained the rationale behind it: 'I trained in South Africa in early 2019. There are a lot of top javelin throwers who travel to South Africa for training. Everyone there is focused on their training, so it helps us understand and work on techniques with fellow athletes. The weather was right for training in South Africa, the training equipment and facilities are very impressive, and the diet is looked after well too.'[136]

Therefore, Neeraj's comeback was remarkable. With a throw of 87.86 m at the Athletics Central North East (ACNE) League meeting in Potchefstroom, South Africa,

---

[136]Kulkarni, Abhijeet. 'Having Seen the Worst and Best in Last Two Years, Neeraj Chopra Targets Olympics Success', *Scroll.in*, 21 April 2020, https://scroll.in/field/959683/having-seen-the-worst-and-best-in-last-two-years-neeraj-chopra-wants-to-make-chance-count-in-tokyo. Accessed on 29 November 2021.

Neeraj marked his arrival post-injury. His throw improved each time consistently during the event. An ecstatic Neeraj tweeted, 'Feeling super awesome to be back in the competition mode. Thank you, everyone, for your good wishes and supporting me always,'[137]

During his rehabilitation in IIS, NIS Patiala and Potchefstroom, South Africa, this was the most important thing on his mind. In his words, 'This was a major target for me during my rehabilitation and I am happy to have qualified for Tokyo.' Notably, this was his second-best throw after his 88.06 m at the Asian Games.[138]

The previous year was a tough one, and this was a step ahead from there. He competed without much expectations and gave it his best. He said to *The Telegraph*, 'To be frank, I was pleasantly surprised. Everyone knew it was a good throw. After the second and third throws went off well, I thought of going for the 85-m mark in the fourth. The jerk and the follow-through came out quite well in the fourth throw, and I knew it was a good one.'[139]

---

[137] PTI. 'Neeraj Chopra Qualifies for Olympics with 87.86m Throw on Comeback', *BusinessLine*, 29 January 2020, https://www.thehindubusinessline.com/news/sports/neeraj-chopra-qualifies-for-olympics-with-8786m-throw-on-comeback/article30682962.ece. Accessed on 29 November 2021.

[138] Roy, Angshuman. '87.86m Throw a Surprise: Neeraj Chopra', *The Telegraph*, 29 January 2020, https://www.telegraphindia.com/sports/87-86m-throw-a-surprise-neeraj-chopra/cid/1740621. Accessed on 29 November 2021.

[139] Ibid.

This was a great improvement. Hence, the training process continued with Klaus and Ishan Marwaha in South Africa. Back then, however, he had no idea that the world would go into lockdown mode. He hoped to participate more in high-intensity competitions to prepare before the Olympics.

∞

From South Africa, Neeraj headed to Antalya, Turkey. Since he could not extend his visa, Neeraj and Rohit Yadav, his training partner, left South Africa. Other throwers at the camp Shivpal, Annu and Vipin continued in South Africa.

'We were not able to extend his visa. But we managed to find another opportunity for Neeraj. He, along with German biomechanics expert Dr Klaus Bartonietz and a physiotherapist, will go to Antalya, Turkey by mid-February and will train there for three to four weeks. They will be back in India by mid-March to participate in the Federation Cup. We have booked the hotel and everything and are waiting for a visa,' AFI's High-Performance Director Volker Herrmann shared.[140]

---

[140] Sankar, Vimal T.N. 'Neeraj Chopra Set for Turkish Sojourn after Visa Issues in South Africa', *The Indian Express*, 8 February 2020, https://www.newindianexpress.com/sport/other/2020/feb/08/neeraj-chopra-set-for-turkish-sojourn-after-visa-issues-in-south-africa-2100558.html. Accessed on 29 November 2021.

It was also decided that Neeraj would not take part in any competitions. It was purely a training camp. The most important event in 2020 would be the Olympics, and Neeraj had to work on correcting a few technical errors in his throw. The idea was to fine-tune the technique and recover, and prepare for the big game.[141]

The training camp in Turkey, however, was curtailed. AFI President Adille Sumariwalla told IANS in March 2020 that the federation had decided to bring back the two contingents in the wake of the rising concerns over the spread of the coronavirus.[142]

༄

Injury-wala time yaad karke, yeh time theek lagta hai. Tab toh main sirf bed pe hi pada rehta tha (Remembering the timer I was injured, this seems better. Then I was just lying in bed).'[143]

Due to the global pandemic, Neeraj had to abandon his camp in Turkey and return to NIS, Patiala. He spent the first

---

[141] Ibid.

[142] IANS. 'Neeraj Chopra, Shivpal Singh to Return from Turkey, South Africa after Covid-19 Travel Advisory', *India Today*, 17 March 2020, https://www.indiatoday.in/sports/other-sports/story/neeraj-chopra-shivpal-singh-to-return-from-turkey-south-africa-after-covid-19-travel-advisory-1656492-2020-03-17. Accessed on 29 November 2021.

[143] Kamath, Amit. 'Neeraj Chopra Says Past 14 Days in Self-Isolation Seem Fine Compared to Injury-Plagued 2019', *Firstpost*, 1 April 2020, https://www.firstpost.com/sports/neeraj-chopra-says-past-14-days-in-self-isolation-seem-fine-compared-to-injury-plagued-2019-8215571.html. Accessed on 29 November 2021.

two weeks in isolation at the camp. When asked about how he felt about this disruption, Neeraj was clear that this was much better than what he saw at the same time last year.

In self-isolation, access to the gymnasium was limited. A training video on the star's Instagram handle shows how he innovated and kept himself fit. He threw different weight balls to work on his throws. He used a slackline wire to work on his balance and core stability. Added to it were push-ups, crawls, pull-ups, high-jumps and the hostel staircase for cardio exercises.

The camp also adopted numerous rules and regulations to keep things in order. Athletes were asked not to share javelins. At the gymnasium, the equipment was segregated. After each training session, the equipment had to be sanitized. Further, the AFI restricted movements of athletes ensuring the best interest of the players in the wake of the pandemic.[144]

Neeraj, however, approached the lockdown and postponement of the Games differently. He commented, 'The fact that now there's one more year to prepare for the Tokyo Olympics is great news for me. I can fine-tune technical aspects.'[145]

After a gap of two months, Neeraj began his outdoor training. He invested his time working on his core strength, and ensuring that he did not gain weight. As the first

---

[144]Ibid.
[145]Ibid.

COVID-19 lockdown in India eased, practice restarted. In July, however, Neeraj had to leave the national preparatory camp at NIS. This was due to some urgent work at home.[146] According to the AFI Standard Operating Procedure, any athlete leaving the camp would have to undergo a 14-day mandatory quarantine before entering the campus.

※

In September the same year, Johannes Vetter made the second-best throw in the history of a new javelin—97.76 m at the Continental Tour Gold. This bettered Neeraj's best throw by nine metres.[147] Around the same time, Neeraj suffered an ankle injury, but it was not serious and he recovered quickly.

Soon as he recovered, the intensity of his training increased. Neeraj had by now become a crucial Indian hope for a medal at the Tokyo Olympics. He was also a TOPS athlete, and hence, no stone was left unturned. Every move, every step had to be taken with utmost caution.

In December, the team of javelin throwers shifted their base to Bhubaneswar. At the Kalinga Stadium, the temperatures

---

[146] Singh, Navneet. 'Javelin Thrower Neeraj Chopra Leaves Patiala Camp', *Hindustan Times*, 12 July 2020, https://www.hindustantimes.com/other-sports/javelin-thrower-neeraj-chopra-leaves-patiala-camp/story-O5Xg5dNFmJsg9Uwa5EkAxI.html. Accessed on 29 November 2021.

[147] 'German Javelin Star Puts Pressure on Neeraj Chopra with 2nd Best Throw in History', *The Bridge*, 7 September 2020, https://thebridge.in/athletics/german-javelin-star-puts-pressure-neeraj-chopra-with-2nd-best-throw-history/. Accessed on 29 November 2021.

were moderate compared to Patiala. Accompanied by Annu Rani, Rohit Yadav, Rajinder Singh and coaches Uwe Hohn and Klaus, the training continued in full flow.

Said Neeraj, 'We are here to train for the Olympics 2020. In 2017 (Asian Championships), I won gold here and have fond memories of the city. With our best efforts, we are hoping to do well at the Olympics.'[148]

Tokyo Beckons

Early in 2021, Neeraj was training in Bhubaneswar. Although the country was still in crisis, Neeraj's sole focus was on training. There was just so much negativity around. In May 2021, Neeraj spoke in an interaction organized by SAI, 'I have shut out all the news from outside because you only hear of COVID cases, and it becomes disturbing. There is a negative atmosphere in the country with the number of cases and people dying. But I am trying to stay focused on my preparation for the Olympics.'[149]

---

[148]PTI. 'Neeraj Chopra and Other Javelin Throwers Begin Training in Bhubaneswar', *The Times of India*, 5 December 2020, https://timesofindia.indiatimes.com/sports/more-sports/athletics/neeraj-chopra-and-other-javelin-throwers-begin-training-in-bhubaneswar/articleshow/79584383.cms. Accessed on 29 November 2021.

[149]Krishnan, Vivek. 'Need More International Competitions before Olympics, Says Star Javelin Thrower Neeraj Chopra', *The New Indian Express*, 12 May 2021, https://www.newindianexpress.com/sport/other/2021/may/12/need-more-international-competitions-before-olympics-says-star-javelin-thrower-neeraj-chopra-2301738.html. Accessed on 29 November 2021.

Neeraj last attended competitions abroad around two years ago, if one ignores the South Africa stint where he qualified for the Tokyo Olympics. In the run-up to Tokyo, he was vocal about his requirements. In a session, Neeraj said, 'It is very important to get high-intensity competition against the top throwers of the world before the Olympics, so I need to play in at least six international competitions before Tokyo. I also need to give time for recovery and training. So, the events have to be spaced out to maybe one or two big events every month.'[150]

It is rather critical for top athletes to get themselves in the groove, in a competitive mode. He rued, 'International competitions help you know where you stand among other athletes. Without them, what is the point of training so much? You cannot just keep training here and expect to be at your best at the Olympics on the very first occasion.'[151]

Moreover, Patiala gets very hot in the summers. Competitions abroad would help him train better. It

---

[150] Roy, Avishek. 'Need High-Intensity Meets to Prepare for Tokyo: Neeraj Chopra', *Hindustan Times*, 25 January 2021, https://www.hindustantimes.com/sports/olympics/need-high-intensity-meets-to-prepare-for-tokyo-neeraj-chopra-101611554356862.html. Accessed on 29 November 2021.

[151] Krishnan, Vivek. 'Need More International Competitions before Olympics, Says Star Javelin Thrower Neeraj Chopra', *The New Indian Express*, 12 May 2021, https://www.newindianexpress.com/sport/other/2021/may/12/need-more-international-competitions-before-olympics-says-star-javelin-thrower-neeraj-chopra-2301738.html. Accessed on 29 November 2021.

would save him from fatigue or even tiring himself before the Olympics. Nobody wanted that. As the progression required, a player's best must emerge during the competing seasons. Here, that was the Olympic Games.

༄

March 2021 Indian Grand Prix

At the Indian Grand Prix-3 at NIS Patiala, Neeraj got back into the competition mode after a year of COVID-19 restrictions. The TOPS athlete bettered his own record with a throw of 88.07 m and won the gold in the process. Representing Haryana at the IGP, Neeraj said post-win, 'I was prepared, and today it was windy. I used my favourite javelin, which helped me. The pandemic did affect training and preparation, but we managed to hold on.'[152]

༄

Two contrasting things were happening in his mind. Observing top athletes from the world, it was clear that Neeraj had to better himself anyhow. Vetter, Rohler, Andreas Hofmann and Magnus Kirt—all had 90-m plus

---

[152]PTI. 'Indian Grand Prix III: Neeraj Chopra Breaks His Own National Record with Throw of 88.07m', *Firstpost*, 5 March 2021, https://www.firstpost.com/sports/indian-grand-prix-neeraj-chopra-breaks-his-own-national-record-with-throw-of-88-07m-9382341.html. Accessed on 29 November 2021.

throws. If Neeraj had to bring back a medal, he had to improve on his throws. Neeraj was indeed in range. If his throws were straighter and did not take as much flight, it could cross the 90-m mark in the sector. Still, Neeraj recognized that the javelin was a very technical and typical sport. A lot of things could go wrong, reducing the range of the javelin. Hence, he agreed that the sole focus should be on oneself, one's own performance.[153]

༄

As the dates to the Olympics drew closer, Neeraj began focusing more on when and how to peak his performance. In June, Neeraj found himself in Lisbon. Here he appeared in an event and won gold with a throw of 83.18 m. Notably, this was not his 100 per cent. He was performing with a training mindset on the coach's recommendations. After his stay in Lisbon till 19 June, Neeraj moved to Sweden to train.

Here, the young champion competed at the Karlstad Grand Prix, a World Athletics Continental Tour Bronze event, at Karlstad, Sweden. With a mediocre throw of 80.96 m, Neeraj won the gold. Explained Manish Malhotra,

---

[153] Roy, Avishek. 'Need High-Intensity Meets to Prepare for Tokyo: Neeraj Chopra', *Hindustan Times*, 25 January 2021, https://www.hindustantimes.com/sports/olympics/need-high-intensity-meets-to-prepare-for-tokyo-neeraj-chopra-101611554356862.html. Accessed on 29 November 2021.

JSW Sports' head of sports excellence, 'It's 13 degrees, rain and wind...so very difficult conditions.'[154]

Kurortane Games

After the Karlstad Grand Prix, another high-profile event followed in Finland. Ahead of the clash, media outlets from all over had dubbed it a pre-Olympics showdown. The reason was that Johannes Vetter and Neeraj Chopra were both competing in the same event. The meet was part of the World Athletics Continental Tour Bronze series and Motonet GP series.

To make it all look more dramatic, pictures of Vetter and Chopra travelling together floated all across. JSW Sports' official Twitter handle tweeted: 'Two of the most exciting prospects in the Javelin world, Junior World Record holder, @Neeraj_chopra1 and the person who has thrown the second farthest javelin in history, @jojo_javelin shared a ride to Finland to compete at the Kuortane Games tomorrow! #BetterEveryday.'[155]

The results were as expected. Neeraj won the bronze medal with an 86.79 m throw. Johannes Vetter won the

---

[154]Rayan, Stan. 'Neeraj Chopra Wins Gold in Sweden', *Sportstar*, 22 June 2021, https://sportstar.thehindu.com/athletics/neeraj-chopra-gold-medal-karlstad-gp-sweden-athletics-meet-tokyo-olympics/article34915966.ece. Accessed on 29 November 2021.

[155]@JWSports, 24 June 2021, Twitter, https://twitter.com/jswsports/status/1407929546108596224?ref_src=twsrc%5Etfw. Accessed on 29 November 2021.

gold and London 2012 gold medallist Keshorn Walcott of Trinidad and Tobago won a silver. Notably, Vetter threw a massive 93.59-m throw. Neeraj's distance was good but not on par with his personal best earlier in the year. Moreover, it was not good enough against the best in the world.

∽

Regardless, Neeraj was all set for the Games. His mindset had been clear from early on—deliver your best and leave the rest to fate. The focus must be on giving his best performance and not worrying about the competition. Medals were secondary. They would happen if Neeraj produced his best, and other faltered.

Before the Games, Prime Minister Narendra Modi organized a session with the athletes heading to the Olympics. Interacting with Neeraj, Modi said, 'I have been told that you got injured, but still you created a new record. You don't need to get bogged down by expectations, don't take the burden of expectations, just focus on your goal.'

Neeraj responded, 'I am focusing on my game. Anything I want, the government is helping me in that. We have a limited career because of injury, I lost some time but I was fully focused on the Olympics. Because of COVID-19, Olympics got postponed, but I kept on preparing for the event.'[156]

---

[156]'Tokyo Olympics: Don't Get Bogged Down by Expectations, PM Modi Tells Javelin Thrower Neeraj Chopra', ANI, 13 July 2021, https://

The expectations were high and the competition was well prepared. In an interaction with select international media organized by World Athletics, Vetter said, 'He (Chopra) threw good throws twice this year. Above 86 m in Finland. If he is healthy and if he is in the right shape, especially in his technique, he can throw far... But he has to fight with me. I am looking to throw over 90 m in Tokyo, so it will be tough for him to beat me.'[157]

Vetter's confidence was in the right place. He was the only man in the world to have thrown beyond 90 m in the past two years. He even reached touching distance to the world record last year, just 72 cm shy of Jan Zelezny!

He added, 'Javelin throw is difficult, the technique is very tough. Everything has to come together. The wind condition will have to be perfect; the surface will have to be perfect, and the technique... You have to think over all angles, speed, etc. I know I am actually in very good shape, but I don't want to put that much pressure on myself. I just want to enjoy such a high-level competition.'[158]

---

www.aninews.in/news/sports/others/tokyo-olympics-dont-get-bogged-down-by-expectations-pm-modi-tells-javelin-thrower-neeraj-chopra20210713173759/. Accessed on 29 November 2021.

[157]"Tokyo 2020: Neeraj Chopra Is Good but Tough for Him to Beat Me, Says German Javelin Thrower Johannes Vetter", *India Today*, 22 July 2021, https://www.indiatoday.in/sports/tokyo-olympics/story/tokyo-olympics-2020-johannes-vetter-on-neeraj-chopra-it-will-be-tough-for-him-to-beat-me-1831250-2021-07-22. Accessed on 29 November 2021.

[158]Ibid.

The Olympics became a big buzz in India as well as the world. The wrestlers, boxers, archers and shooters were a disappointment. There were some flickers of hope but let's concentrate on Neeraj Chopra's game.

Owing to the global pandemic, which was still prevalent, the Indian contingent reached Tokyo in batches. According to the Games protocol, athletes could enter Tokyo only five days before their event and leave no later than 48 hours after their competition ended. There were also quarantine rules and regulations for different players that proved a tremendous logistical challenge for the IOA. Neeraj was in Upsala, Sweden, before the Games and went to Tokyo from there.[159]

7 August 2021

> *'Yeh kya ho gaya, Bhai'*
> (What has happened, Brother?)
>
> —Neeraj Chopra[160]

---

[159]'First Batch of Indian Olympics Squad to Leave for Tokyo on July 17', *Hindustan Times*, 6 July 2021, https://www.hindustantimes.com/sports/others/first-batch-of-indian-olympics-squad-to-leave-for-tokyo-on-july-17-101625592083826.html. Accessed on 29 November 2021.

[160]Dhar, Pulasta. 'How Neeraj Chopra Beat a Serious Injury on His Road to Gold', *Mint Lounge*, 12 August 2021, https://lifestyle.livemint.com/health/fitness/how-neeraj-chopra-beat-a-serious-injury-on-his-road-to-gold-111628685357804.html. Accessed on 29 November 2021.

On the evening of 7 August, the best from the qualifying rounds had gathered in the national stadium. Former Olympic gold medallist Thomas Roehler had opted out of the Games. The other two medallists, Yago and Walcott were out in the qualifiers.

Vetter delivered a disappointing performance in the qualifiers, losing out on his winning streak of 18. The national stadium was lit. Neeraj was in form. He had often said that his best performances were in the biggest of events. The more limelight, competition and challenges he faced, the better were his efforts and, ultimately, performance.

The temperature was 28 degrees, humidity 81 per cent and the wind was blowing east at a speed of 2 km/hr. The stage was set. There was a slight breeze, and there were prospects of rain. The commentators were right in noticing the weather. If it rained, it could wreak havoc on the performance of the athletes.

The javelin boots have high spikes to control the body from that blocking leg, after the athlete makes his full-effort throw. There were two 23-year olds, including Neeraj, and a 38-year-old. But time and again, the commentators reminded the audience watching the Games worldwide that the best prospect and champion was Johannes Vetter. Nobody else in the finals had thrown over 90 m.

The list was as follows:

S. No.	Country	Athlete	Age	PB	SB
1	Moldova	Andrian Mardare	26	86.66 m	86.66 m
2	India	Neeraj Chopra	23	88.07 m	88.07 m
3	Sweden	Kim Amb	31	86.49 m	82.40 m
4	Romania	Alexandru Mihatia Novac	24	86.37 m	83.27 m
5	Czechoslovakia	Vitezslav Vesely	38	88.34 m	83.04 m
6	Germany	Julian Weber	26	88.29 m	84.95 m
7	Finland	Lassi Etelatalo	33	84.98 m	84.50 m
8	Germany	Johannes Vetter	28	97.76 m	96.29 m
9	Pakistan	Arshad Nadeem	24	86.38 m	86.38 m
10		Pavel Mialeshka	28	85.06 m	85.06 m
11	Czechoslovakia	Jakub Vadlejch	30	89.73 m	84.39 m
12	Belarus	Aliaksei Katkavets	23	86.05 m	85.10 m

The beautiful pink Panasonic boards welcomed each player in the same sequence. Neeraj entered the competition with a haircut because now nothing could come between him and his best throw. Neeraj jogged in front of the cameras with a bandana holding his hair, joined hands to bow, and did a namaste.

If one sees the season's best performances, Neeraj was only second to Vetter. He entered the ground looking very calm and composed. Remarking on Vetter, the commentators said, 'Here is the great man. JoJo (his nickname), Johannes Vetter. Looking very relaxed and composed. He is an enormous individual, isn't he? Sporting a beard with his hair slicked back.' He was followed by Pakistani Arshad Nadeem who waved and tapped his chest with the flag of his country on his T-shirt.

The Moldavian threw the first one above the 80-m mark. Neeraj followed, wearing a dark blue vest with 'India' marked on the back. The cameras showed him walking up to Arshad Nadeem, taking the fluorescent coloured javelin from him. He rubbed the grip and swiftly walked towards the starting mark. Neeraj looked muscled, a little anxious, but in control.

With the javelin in his right hand, Neeraj ran towards the running track, his start mark. He relaxed his left arm, stopped and dropped his javelin. He then adjusted his lower back brace and picked up the javelin again. He extended his left leg and twisted and stretched his right foot. With the javelin tip wrapped in the left hand and the right hand on the grip, he pulled his arm and shoulder, all the way back. He looked extremely focused.

With the javelin above his shoulder, he ran high and fast towards the throwing arc with good, strong strides. It was a nice crossover. His arm pulled back, and in a split second the javelin was flying through the skies. Just the way his career had been!

The roar was loud. The throw was confident. Neeraj put all of his power into it and landed on his arms. The landing distance: 87.03 m.

Other competitors followed. Another important thing was that there was very little gap in the season's best performances of the athletes other than of course, Vetter. Hence, it came down to who would be giving the best performance on the day. With his throw and the dominating performance in the qualifying round, Neeraj was automatically the next favourite after Vetter.

With bib number 2183, wearing a yellow-and-black-striped vest, Vetter hopped onto his feet at the starting mark. He ran strong and confident, but his first throw was not impressive—82.52 m. Following Vetter's mark, the cameras moved swiftly to Neeraj, who obliged them with a cheerful smile. It seemed as if he knew it. He was relaxed, sipping some water. His job was more or less done. He had set a solid benchmark.

The competition was happening in two rounds. The top eight throwers in the first three attempts would be allowed the remaining three. That essentially meant that if you were good enough, you would qualify for the final of finals.

After his first round, Neeraj started for his second one after the Moldavian improved slightly on his opening attempt. Neeraj walked towards the starting point. He gestured for claps overhead to raise a response from the watching crowd. Confident, he held the javelin in his right hand as the select Indian crowd in the audience was ready to witness the best performance of the day.

Neeraj was not looking for a medal now. He was aiming

for gold. He led in the first round and Vetter was down, languishing five metres behind. Neeraj ran in fast, did the crossover. The javelin flew out of his hands and he did not look towards the sector. He just knew he had bettered the first attempt. The moment the javelin left his hand, he knew he had done it.

Neeraj turned back to the stands, raising his arms. He punched the sky twice and smiled. The throw measured 87.58 m! Even Klaus could not hide his feelings. Others followed with their throws.

Another sight that captured the eye was that of Neeraj, in utmost sportsmanship, clapping as Vetter readied himself to make the throw. Vetter ran hard and fast but right before he made the throw, his left foot slipped. The javelin left Vetter's arm, flew a little distance even as he tumbled, rolling outside the throwing arc. It was a no-throw.

Vetter's frustration was evident. He walked back, still looking at the run-up track. His left foot had slipped, destroying his block. The power failed to transfer, damaging his prospects.

Neeraj's third was not good enough. Vetter's third was also disqualified. Nodding, he stepped out of the throwing arc. He looked at the synthetic turf, utterly disappointed. At the end of three attempts, Vetter was sitting at the disqualification margin. Four throwers had to make an attempt, and anyone could push him down and out. With the last throw from Belarus, Vetter stood ninth in the table. And the commentators were loud and clear, 'He is done.

He is finished in Tokyo 2020.'

Vetter had delivered a disappointing performance. He was fourth in Rio and that was his motivation. How much did it mean to him? He had the Olympics rings tattooed on his back. At the end of the three designated throws, Neeraj led the standings with 87.58 m, followed by Czech Vitezslav Vesely (85.44 m) and German Julian Weber (85.30 m). Arshad Nadeem, who called Neeraj Chopra his hero, was in fourth place.[161]

At the end of the round, officials paused the game for some time as the 1500 m finals was about to start. The performing sequence also changed. The worst performer of the first three rounds went in first and the best performer went in last. Regardless, nobody came close to Neeraj's second throw of 87.58 m. It was his best performance on the day and it won him the gold medal.

Czech Republic's Jakub Vadlejch came second with his best effort of 86.67 m and another Czech Vitezslav Vesely took the bronze with 85.44 m.

The boy from Khandra became a young man in Tokyo. Twenty-three-year-old Neeraj Chopra won India its first gold medal in athletics.

---

[161]Men's Javelin Throw Final–Athletics, Tokyo 2020 Replays, Olympics, https://olympics.com/en/video/men-s-javelin-throw-final-athletics-tokyo-2020-replays. Accessed on 29 November 2021.

Epilogue

'Is se badaa toh shayad hi kuch hoga'
(Maybe there is nothing greater than this.)

With the win in Tokyo, Neeraj became an online sensation and an offline superstar. He was after all the first Indian to win a gold medal at athletics in the Olympics and only second after Abhinav Bindra to win an individual gold. Athletics for the longest time had not been seen as India's strength in the international sporting arena.

There are a few exceptions of course like Anju Bobby George, but the field is only sparsely populated. No doubt that there are many striving to achieve that glory and success but a variety of reasons ensure that only the rarest of the rare gems make it. And in 2021, this gem was Neeraj Chopra.

After his last attempt, it was clear to other competitors as well as Neeraj that he was winning the gold. Right after the last attempt, Neeraj turned around, bowing down on the maroon turf—the turf which turned his life around. Other players came forward and congratulated him and an ecstatic Neeraj received it all with a sense of accomplishment.

He then ran towards the stands where the Indian players, coaches and staff stood cheering for him. Quickly the national flag was passed onto him. Loud cheers reverberated the premises as Neeraj wrapped the flag around his shoulders and ran around on the track in complete joy. He may or may not have an idea of what he had achieved then but in the coming days what happened set the record straight.

The two Czech players who came second and third continued the legacy of Neeraj's YouTube coach Czech javelin thrower Jan Zelezeny. The photographers made them all strike a pose—the two Czechs players on each side and Neeraj with the Indian flag gracing the centre. At the medal ceremony later, dressed in his blue kit, Neeraj stepped on the podium wearing a white mask. He kissed his medal, took it to his forehead with reverence and wore it.

The medal was designed by Junichi Kawanishi and was approximately 3.35 inches in diameter. The medal weighed around 556 g and consisted of about 6.7 g gold and rest of it was silver.[162] [163] Neeraj wore it around his neck and held a small bouquet which had flowers grown in three districts of northeast Japan which were wrecked by the Tohuku earthquake and tsunami of 2011 and the Fukushima nuclear plant disaster.[164] Making it for Neeraj Chopra, a culmination of decade-long journey!

As the Indian national flag rose higher, Neeraj became a source of pride and inspiration for Indians all across the world. One could see him singing the national anthem as it echoed in the premises of the stadium in Tokyo.

He tweeted from his handle after the win: 'Still processing this feeling. To all of India and beyond, thank you so much for your support and blessings that have helped me reach this stage. This moment will live with me forever.'[165]

His victory led a nation-wide jubilation. In a way he had fulfilled the aspirations of the entire Indian sporting

---

[162]Mendoza, Jordan. 'Gold medals not entirely made of gold?' *USA Today*, https://www.usatoday.com/story/sports/olympics/2021/07/22/2020-olympics-tokyo-gold-silver-bronze-medals/8046071002/. Accessed on 9 December 2021.

[163]Woodword, Aylin. 'Tokyo Olympics Medals: Composition, Weight, Amount of Gold', *Insider*, https://www.insider.com/tokyo-olympics-medals-composition-weight-amount-gold-2021-7. Accessed on 9 December 2021.

[164]'Tokyo Olympics 2020: Here's the Significance of Victory Bouquets Awarded to Medalists', *News 18*, https://www.news18.com/news/buzz/tokyo-olympics-2020-heres-the-significance-of-victory-bouquets-awarded-to-medalists-4038890.html. Accessed on 9 December 2021.

[165]https://twitter.com/neeraj_chopra1/status/1424297067166408705?lang=en.

ecosystem which had been striving hard to get gold at Olympics. These players tweeted out with utmost pride and joy lauding Neeraj's efforts. He had not flown to India yet but his fan base had increased multifold and fan pages on social media were up and running.

Prime Minister Narendra Modi called and congratulated him on his victory and from then on till early next morning Neeraj was on back-to-back calls and interviews. News channels clamored for interviews and bites from him. It was amusing to find that many of those interviewing him had very little knowledge of the game and the questions were mostly centred around how he felt after winning the gold medal.

Similar questions were asked to family back in India where a giant screen was installed in his village to watch the final game. The village was thronged by thousands of people. Sweets were distributed and dhol walas ensured that it was a party in the vicinity. When Neeraj slept after a long night of interviews, he kept his medal right by his side. He flew out from Tokyo with other Indian players like Ravi Dahiya, another medal winner, and Vinesh Phogat. In Delhi, Neeraj was received like a hero. Thousands had thronged the Indira Gandhi Airport where the flight landed. Amidst tight security and a sea of people, Neeraj came out flashing his medal in one hand making a powerful statement. It was the prince's homecoming!

A beautiful thing happened there too. Neeraj found some known faces, including Sunny who later accompanied

Neeraj out to the receptions laid out for him. Over the course of the next two months, Neeraj's life transformed. From meetings, engagements, receptions, endorsements etc., he was invited everywhere. Being the humble person he is, he recognized the importance of respecting the love he was receiving. At the felicitation ceremony with the sports minister Anurag Singh Thakur, Neeraj said, '*Yeh medal mera nahin, poore India ka hai* (this is not my medal alone, but of the entire country)'. Notably, each of those interactions was well recorded in pictures and videos and they were online in no time through his fan club pages and handles. Soon, his number of online followers skyrocketed. Within a day of winning the medal his Instagram followers increased by 1.1 million.[166] This kept on increasing.

In a month's time, according to a report by YouGov SPORT, Neeraj's interactions had risen to 12.79 million. He also became the most mentioned athlete globally on Instagram during the Tokyo Olympics. This added to his rising brand value. Business Insider in mid-September 2021 wrote, 'Since the day on which Chopra won the Olympic Gold, his stock has skyrocketed on social and digital media. As per the report, Neeraj Chopra recorded over 2.9 million mentions from over 1.4 million authors, making him the

---

[166]'Here's how many crores Tokyo Olympics gold medalist Neeraj Chopra will earn every year from endorsements', *DNA*, https://www.dnaindia.com/sports/report-here-s-how-many-crores-tokyo-olympics-gold-medalist-neeraj-chopra-will-earn-every-year-from-endorsements-2913339. Accessed on 9 December 2021.

'most mentioned' athlete globally on Instagram during the 2020 Tokyo Olympics... As a result, Neeraj Chopra's reach on social and digital media has reached a staggering 412 million, spanning several geographies over the world. These numbers have combined to take the athlete's social media valuation to a total of ₹428 crore.'[167]

Then there came the prize money. As cash rewards Neeraj received ₹6 crore from the Manohar Lal Khattar-led Haryana government, Punjab government gave ₹2 crore as special cash reward, BCCI gave ₹1 crore with an additional crore from the IPL franchise Chennai Super Kings. Byju's announced a ₹2 crore cash reward and JSW group announced ₹1 crore reward. When a fan suggested 'Xuv 700 for him' on Twitter, Anand Mahindra responded, 'Yes indeed. It will be my privilege & honour to gift our Golden Athlete an XUV 700@rajesh664 @vijaynakra Keep one ready for him please.' Soon a beautiful car was delivered. The number plate and customized insignia on the black chassis of the vehicle was 8758.[168] The list of rewards kept adding up and then there were the brand endorsements.

---

[167]'Neeraj Chopra's social media valuation rises to Rs 428 crore: JSW Sports', *Business Insider*, https://www.businessinsider.in/advertising/brands/article/neeraj-chopra-social-media-valuation-rose-to-rs-428-cr/articleshow/86199084.cms. Accessed on 9 December 2021.

[168]'Raining rewards for Neeraj Chopra: A list of cash awards for Olympic gold medallist', *The Indian Express*, https://indianexpress.com/article/olympics/raining-rewards-for-neeraj-chopra-full-list-of-cash-awards-given-to-indias-olympic-gold-medallist-7443557/. Accessed on 9 December 2021.

Now that Neeraj was a household name, brands clamored for signing him as an ambassador. Most of these engagements were taken care of by JSW who had been engaged with him since a long time. JSW's professional support helped Neeraj bag best deals. Further, all of it had to be taken care of along with Neeraj's tight training schedule. Moreover, his fees had increased tenfold. As I write this, Neeraj has over 703,500 followers on Twitter with over 5.1 million fans on Instagram. All of this is monetized well, keeping his audience well engaged with the star who has risen from limited means. Posts about his life, cars, flashy products, pictures with fans, dancing at his physiotherapist Ishan's wedding or even being rewarded at numerous functions keep cropping up; Neeraj is religiously followed by his fan base.

His family has also been significantly impacted. Everyone wants a picture with the Panipat boy who made India proud. Local administration, politicians etc., are also not far in line when Neeraj comes home. The family is now famous all across. The *baithak* is now known to everybody.

During his sister's wedding in November, famous sportspersons and known politicians were invited. Haryana chief minister Manohar Lal Khattar visited the family to bless the daughter and so did the former CM Bhupinder Singh Hooda who had played a critical role in giving a fillip to sports in the state. Along came a big stream of politicians and sports stars. It was quite 'lit' on Instagram, as one would say.

Well, through it all, Neeraj stays a humble person, doing everything he can in the time he has and touching lives wherever he goes. Recently, he received the highest sports award in the country, Major Dhyan Chand Khel Ratna Award. And, in pursuance of Prime Minister Narendra Modi's clarion call to the olympians and paralympians, Neeraj met students from 75 schools at Sanskardham in Ahmedabad. The idea was to promote balanced diet, fitness, sports and more.

∾

In a nutshell, Neeraj has had a wonderful journey so far. He has kept utmost focus throughout, learnt lessons at every step and adopted ways that can help him do better. He has found love in javelin and given all of himself to it. When all of it fell in place, Neeraj shone as the brightest star in the sky. Through it all, he has tried to maintain utmost balance, managing the stardom along with being the grounded self that he most relates with. He has also had the fortune of meeting great friends and mentors in his life who have helped his excel in his trade.

Monu magic is something that reflects in conversations with Neeraj's uncles quite often. Monu met Neeraj early in his life when he picked the sport and since then he has in his own way guarded Neeraj from all the challenges that he has faced. He took on the role of a coach but before that he has been a friend and brother-like figure to Neeraj. The

Chopra family treats him as their own. People like Monu helped Neeraj stay on track and fulfill the dream of a family, his friends in sports circle, coaches, mentors and the entire nation of over one billion people.

Furthermore, Neeraj has his goals clear. A Diamond League medal and the Paris Olympics await. Hopefully his success breaks the mould and India sees many gold medalists making it proud world over. In words of Neeraj, on Independence Day, '...As an athlete and a soldier, my heart is full of emotion when I see the national flag flying high. Jai Hind.'[169]

---

[169]https://twitter.com/neeraj_chopra1/status/1426789967657795584

Acknowledgments

Haryana is my home state and I know that the state's best days are yet to come. And hence, the book is credited to Haryanvis and Indians all across fighting daily to better themselves in the field of their choosing.

This book is a product of numerous stories shared with utmost honesty by many people. It also has the support of people who wish well for me and have seen me striving hard to make an impact. I thank Vivek Chaudhary who has been a kind friend and keeps alive the old principles of integrity in public service. I also thank journalist and friend Shagun who is seeing a tough phase in life but meets every day with a big smile. Also thanks to Sunny 'Sardar' who runs his business in Panipat with large heartedness. Then there are numerous people I met at his store on Ring Road, Panipat. Thank you for the conversations and laughter.

I would also like to thank Parvinder Singh, Rajinder Singh, Baba Coach, Jitender Jaglan, Kashinath Naik, Olympian and champion thrower Shivpal. Thank you,

Deepak Ahluwalia, successful sportsman and a remarkable man in service. Tales he shares, make for a wonderful book waiting to be written.

Thanks are also due to the Chopra clan! Having met and spoken to them many times now; I see how Neeraj's success comes from lessons he had been taught early on. The family lives together as a strong unit and I wish them good health, happiness and prosperity. Particularly, thanking the brothers, Satish, Bhim, Surender and Sultan; who have shared their stories and life with such passion. Also, thank you for the cups of tea and dinner.

I would also like to thank Yashvir Kadian Bhaiya, Yudhvir Khyaliya Uncle and Satya Dadiji for all the support. Thank you, Sanjeev Sanyal for the encouragement. Thank you, Ravi Ladva for your help with early research. Thanks are also due to my friends Astik Sinha and Upasna Singh. I am grateful to Indic Academy and its founder Hari Kiran Vadlamani for creating an ecosystem of book reading with the Indic Book club. There are many others who helped me with their perspectives and opinions. I thank each one of you.

Thank you, my commissioning editor and friend, Yamini Chowdhury, Mohan Sinha, Sakschi Verma and Amrita Chakravorty for taking care of the project. I also thank my kunba (family) and rishtedaari (relations). My grandfather Shri Vijay Kumar was deputy commissioner in Panipat when he pushed for development work of the Shivaji Stadium in the early 1990s. A stone plaque in the right corner of the stadium remembers his contributions. It has been his passion for Haryana that has motivated me for years. I would like to whole-heartedly thank my parents, Mr Gunvir Singh and Mrs Anita Kadian. Thank you for everything. I am because you are! Thank you, Anirudh for accompanying me in my ventures and being a solid support. Regards are also due to my in-laws Mrs Shuchi and Mr Ashok Sur and their daughter Suranya. And a very special thanks to my friend and now wife, Suhelika.

www.ingramcontent.com/pod-product-compliance
Lightning Source LLC
Chambersburg PA
CBHW020231170426
43201CB00007B/387